C.

MW01595729

One Night In Atlanta

Gleefullly twists and turns, it's
a nifty read with a surprise ending.

Book Critics.org

Fans of the 'LateShift' Mysteries
will take delight in the surprising
twist.

Denver book club

A real page turner, this is a book
you won't want to put down.

Katereads.com

Also by Donna Gardner

Stalker

Seven Days

The Wedding

Donna Gardner

One Night in Atlanta

A 'Ross and Company' Novel

Published in the United States

Instant publishing (Fundcraft)

ISBN 978-1-60458-674-9 $9.99

9 781604 586749

5 0 9 9 9

For my daughter

Stephanie

The most effective medicine here
on earth is love unconditional.

- Sri Chinmoy

One Night in Atlanta

Prologue

"What the……?" He didn't even finish the sentence before he hit the ground.

"Take that you stupid cocksucker," his assailant screamed before kicking him in the face. Once, twice, then he spit on him and walked away.

The pain was so excruciating

he could barely move and he felt something dripping down his face, blood he assumed.

The squat little Italian that he worked for came strutting down the alley toward him in his shiny three piece suit.

"Wassa matta witt chu?" He shouted in his employee's face. "gettup."

"I don't need anymore of this shit Gino," he replied as he spit some blood out of his mouth, "I am done fighting you're battles, I'm not a bouncer, I'm the guy that takes the punches for you. I quit."

Waving his hands Gino laughed, "you're on parole, you can't quit, fucka you, I killa couple 'o guys like you once."

Rolling into a sitting position he gave a short laugh, " sure you did Gino, sure you did."

Groaning he slowly stood up. "You might have to kill a couple more then cause you're on your own." Using his sleeve to wipe some blood from his mouth, he turned to look at his now former boss. His left eye was already beginning to swell and his vision was slightly impaired.

As he staggered down the street toward his car he could hear Gino screaming at him. "Fucka youthen, don' comebackahere, I'ma warnin' you."

He practically fell into the drivers seat of his old Toyota, it felt good though to rest his head on the steering wheel and as he gingerly touched the side of his face he wondered what he was going to do now.

Grimacing in pain he reached into his pocket and fished out his cell phone. Looking through the address book he found the number he was looking for, he hesitated then punched in the number. As it began to ring he thought better of it and disconnected the call.

Leaning back he winced again then thought about his options, *I have no choice.* Reaching for the phone again he hit redial.

One ring, two, three, he almost hoped the call would go unanswered

"Yeah?"

He jumped when he heard the voice and for a second was at a loss for words.

"Hello," the voice said, louder now, impatient.

"Hey it's me," he said in a ragged breathe.

Silence for a moment. "Didn't expect to hear from you again."

"Things change."

Short laugh. That miserable evil laugh that he'd come to despise. Pausing for a moment he took a deep breathe and told him if he was interested he may have a plan.

"Yeah?"

He could hear the doubt in his voice. "Something that could put some money in our pockets," he told him, "and a little bit of pay back at the same time."

"Keep talking," the devil replied.

Book One

Donna and Isaura
The Journey

I have learned not to think little of anyone's belief no matter how strange it may be. I have tried to keep an open mind and it is not the ordinary things that could close it but the strange things, the extra-ordinary things that make one wonder if they be mad or sane.

- Bram stoker

Four months later

1

"*A*untie Donna pleeeease stay." Hannah begged.

Grinning down at her two year old god daughter Donna got back down on the floor beside her. Pulling her on her lap she began to tickle her.

"Nooooo," Hannah screamed loving every second of it. "Anna ticko you."

Donna chuckled as the little girl began pinching the sides of her stomach. Playing along she started to laugh. "No Hanah no," she begged.

The little girl collapsed in a fit of giggles.

Giving her one more hug she told her that she had to go.

"No," Hannah replied with a firm shake of her head.

"I have to go see Uncle Paul, you don't want him to be sad do you?"

"No," she replied pouting. "Me go see Unco Pawwel. Him come home soon?"

Donna's husband Paul was on tour with his band 'LateShift,'

they were promoting their latest album 'One Night in Atlanta.'

Her and the Bass player's wife Isaura were leaving in a couple of hours and were heading to Georgia to meet the band. They were ending their four month tour in the U.S. Capital, their last show would be in the Georgia Dome, a sold out show with over 51,000 fans.

"He's coming home very soon," Donna told Hannah, "and we'll come and visit you, would you like that?" She asked getting up off the floor.

Nodding, Hannah stuck her finger in her mouth and her eyes filled with tears.

Turning to her mother Amy, Donna looked at her in a silent plea for help.

Scooping her daughter up in her arms she told Hannah that they would walk Auntie Donna to her truck.

"When will you be back?" Amy asked.

"Isaura and I are leaving today, the concert is the day after tomorrow and we'll head home the day after. "LateShift' should be back the following day."

"Are they glad that the tour is almost over?'

"I think so," Donna replied. "It must be hard being on that tour bus 24/7 with three other guys and Paul sounds tired."

"When will Ben be back?"

Amy sighed. "He was supposed to be home over a week ago but they held him back, hopefully he will be able to get out sometime in the next few day."

Ben was a journalist, very well known and in huge demand. He had quit his job about a year ago and was now freelancing. He was making a pile of money, the only problem was, he away more often than he was at home.

His work to him to war zones and other parts of the world that were devastated by nature and man himself, but Ben seemed to thrive on danger. Certainly he was always looking for the next adventure.

Donna and the band 'LateShift' had become acquainted with Ben a few years ago, he was working as an unpaid intern for a local newspaper over the summer. He had been sent to interview the band who was performing at an outdoor concert on Canada Day. Circumstances had Ben right at the scene as two men tried to kill the members of the band by detonating a bomb on the stage that the band was performing on.

His coverage of that incident garnered him two awards and nationwide attention.

A year later the band chose him to accompany them to the Bahamas, he would produce a documentary about the making of their first album.

Coincidentally Canadian super star Harmon Carter was kidnapped and it had been Ben's film footage that had led him, Donna and Isaura, the bass players wife to the celebrity. The three of them risked their lives to res

cue the singer and by the time Ben had returned to Canada he him- self was a celebrity and a highly sought after journalist. He was soon fielding job offers from all
over the world.

Then three years ago he and his fiancé Amy had gotten marr- ied on a cruise ship. It was a we- dding that had almost not taken place. With only one day before the ceremony was to take place Amy had told Ben she didn't want to get married. Then in an odd twist the woman who had been Amy's nanny disappeared.

Donna quickly realized that the two events were related and set out on a frantic twelve hour mission to find out who was be- hind it. In a complicated and bizarre twist she discovered that Bens' mother and his recently paroled uncle had conspired to stop the wedding from taking happening.

Ben and Amy did get married as planned and Donna was also able to rescue the nanny too.

In gratitude they had named their first child after Donna, so Hannah shared her middle name with her god mother.

"As soon as Ben gets back we'll have you and Paul over, we can have dinner and get caught up."

"We would really love that," Donna replied giving her a hug.

"Anna go wiff Auntie Donna?"

"Not this time sweetie," Amy told her daughter. "Give Auntie Donna a hug goodbye."

Putting on her biggest pout

she nodded and flung her ams around Donna's neck.

It took a moment to unravel herself from Hannah's grip, then she jumped into her truck and waved to both of them as she turned around and headed down the long winding driveway.

With her suitcase already packed and in the truck she was now on her way to Oshawa to pick up Isaura. They would be heading to Michigan and planned to stop in Milan, there they were going to have dinner and stay the night with close friends of Donna's.

They would continue on their journey leaving early tomorrow morning and planned to arrive in Atlanta late afternoon.

Donna could hardly wait to see her husband, it had been a long few months and she was happy that it was almost over. The tour bus was scheduled to arrive in the morning and the two women would be meeting up with their husbands as soon as they got into the city.

2

"*I*'m starving," Isaura told Donna, "I have some coupons for McDonalds."

"We better not eat," Donna replied, "I know Kirk will be making a huge fancy meal and we'll want to have a good appetite."

"Does he do all the cooking?" Isaura asked.

Donna nodded. "Always, as far as I know he's done all of the cooking since the day they married." Thinking back she remembered when they had first met the Straub's.

It was on a cruise ship about a decade ago. They had become fast friends and had gone on a number of cruises after that as well as getting together at each others homes. One summer the Gardners would drive to Michigan, the following year the Straubs would come to Canada.

Donna thought back to three years ago when Ben and Amy's wedding had been in jeopardy, Lisa was right there to help her figure out who had kidnapped the nanny and was terrorizing Amy.

"There's the sign saying we're only six kilometers from the Ambassadors Bridge."

Isaura's voice pulled Donna out of her thoughts. Looking at her watch she told Isaura that they would be at the Straub's in an hour.

It took well over that to get just to get through customs and the traffic was so bad going into Detroit that they wouldn't get to Milan on schedule. No way.

Donna pulled her cell phone out of her purse and called the Straub home.

After explaining that they were caught in traffic and unsure of what time they would arrive

Kirk assured her it wasn't a problem.

"We'll see you when you get here." He told her.

Closing her phone she told Isaura that if all went well they would probably be in Milan with in an hour or so.

"Detroit doesn't look like a very nice place, " Isaura commented as she looked around.

"They have a lot of problems that's for sure, the economy in the US is pretty bad and this city is really feeling it."

"Since we've left Canada it seems a lot rougher and dirtier."

Donna nodded. "The unemployment rate here is really high, and there is a lot of crime, housing is really cheap, you could be an ok house for thirty thousand bucks."

"Really?" Isaura asked. "That cheap?"

"Hard to believe isn't it?" Looking around they both laughed.

"Maybe not," Isaura replied.

"There's our exit," Donna told her companion pointing ahead, "I think we'll be there within a half an hour."

Exiting to the right onto US 23 South they merged into traffic.

"What does that mean?" Isaura asked, pointing to a sign.

"Exactly what it says," Donna told her. "If you kill or injure a person in a construction zone it could get you a 7,500 dollar fine and up to fifteen years in jail."

"I've never heard of anything like that."

"We don't have it in Canada, that's why," Donna explained. "It's a law here in Michigan, named after Andy Lefko, he was a road worker left paralyzed after being struck by a speeding motorist in 1999."

"Don't drive too fast then," Isaura warned, "that's a lot of money."

"It's a lot of jail time," Donna laughed, "I could come up with seventy five hundred bucks." She quickly looked down at her spedometer though, just to be sure she was within the speed limit.

Moments later a green GMC Suburban pulled alongside them. The passenger had the window rolled down and seemed to be waving at Donna.

Ignoring them Donna sped up

slightly, hoping the truck would either pass her or move in be - hind her.

"What are they doing?" Isaura asked sounding worried.

"I don't know," Donna frowned.

The truck kept pace with them and the passenger began gesturing wildly and pointing to the side of her SUV.

Donna lifted her left hand off the steering wheel and with her hand outstretched she shrugged. "What?" She mouthed to the person who appeared to be trying to tell her something.

Pointing again to the side of Donna's Jimmy, she rolled down her window and tried to look out to see if there was something wrong. "I think I had better pull over," she told Isaura.

By the time they were stop-ed at the edge of the highway the green truck was long gone and out of sight.

Both women walked around the truck looking at the tires and for anything else that might be wrong.

"I don't see a problem? Do you?" Donna asked Isaura.

She shook her head, "no, I do-n't think so."

"That's weird," Donna replied with a frown, "they seemed to be trying to tell us something." With one more inspection they got back in the vehicle. "We'll be in Milan in about ten minutes and I'll have Kirk take another look," Donna said.

They had no sooner turned onto Marvin Street and were only a couple of houses from the Straub home when they heard a bang and a clunk.

"What on earth could that be?" Donna asked.

"Oh my god" Isaura screamed, pointing at the hood of the truck, "we're in big trouble."

3

"Jump out," Donna yelled as she slammed on the brakes and quickly threw the transmission into park.

Isaura opened the door and took a flying leap, landing on the grass next to the curb.

Donna wasn't as lucky, with a bang the flames that were licking their way along the edges of hood had now exploded into the front of the truck right under the steering wheel. Before she could get out the bottom of her jeans were on fire.

"Shit," she cursed as she jumped out. Pulling her jacket off she used it to smother the flames that were slowly moving up the leg of her pants.

"Are you okay?" Isaura asked running up to her.

"I think so, thank god for these boots, if I hadn't been wearing them I'd probably have a really bad burn on my leg."

"What's wrong now?" Isaura cried as Donna grimaced and sank to the ground.

"I have to get this boot off I think it's melting on my leg."

"Here let me," Isaura replied as she knelt down and tried to get the boot off without doing any damage.

"Oh oh, here come the troops," Donna said with a short laugh.

Looking in the direction she was nodding, Isaura could see both Kirk and Lisa Straub running toward them.

With a fire extinguisher in hand Kirk quickly began spraying the truck.

Kneeling down beside Donna Lisa asked if she was okay.

"I'll live."

"What happened?"

Shrugging she told her they didn't know. "We heard a weird clunk then a bang then we saw the flames coming out from under the hood."

"Well your boot is totally ruined," Isaura told her, "but your leg doesn't appear to be injured."

"Dang," Lisa laughed playfully, "those are nice boots, that is a real shame. Just think though, you have a reason to go shop - ping."

With a laugh Donna gave her friend a hug, "I'm so happy to see you."

"You won't be taking that thing to Atlanta," Kirk told them as he walked away from Donna's Suv. "I'll tow it into my driveway and take a look at it but I think it is probably a write off."

"Great," Donna replied, "do you have a car rental place here in Milan?"

"You're not renting a car," Lisa told her, "you can take the Jag."

"Really?" Donna said in surprise, "you'd let us take your Jaguar to Georgia?"

"Well yaaa-uh, you may as well go in style."

Giving her a hug Donna told her how grateful she was.

Hours later Isaura and Donna were helping with the cleanup in the Straub kitchen.

"We want to leave here early tomorrow morning, we'd like to get to Atlanta by dark," Donna told Lisa.

"Will the guys be there by then?" Lisa asked as she began putting plates in the cupboard.

"They should be, they have a

concert tonight at the Houston Astrodome and as soon as it's over they'll get on the tour bus and head to Georgia."

Isaura nodded, "then the road-ies will set up for the last show the day after tomorrow."

Donna continued, "they'll be waiting for us tomorrow night, we have rooms at the Four Sea - sons."

"Ooh I'm so jealous, " Lisa laughed. "You must be so excit-ed," how long since you've seen them?"

"Five months," Isaura told her with tears in her eyes, "I can har-dly wait."

"I can't either," Donna admit-ted, "I'm so glad this tour is over, in a few days we'll be home and everything will be back to norm-mal."

Interrupting them Kirk came into the kitchen. "Your truck is a right off, I think you should call your insurance company."

"I will and I'll have it towed out of your driveway as soon I can."

"The two of you look beat," Lisa told Donna and Isaura, "I'll show you your room, if you're leaving that early you need to get to sleep."

With a tired nod Donna agr-eed, "I'm ready for bed."

"Me too," Isaura said with a yawn.

4

*D*onna and Isaura were on the highway by seven the following morning.

"Your truck looked worse this morning than it did last night." Isaura told her.

Shaking her head Donna told her she couldn't believe it. "It's a total mess, I'll call the insurance company in an hour or so." Looking at her watch she figured they would be open by then.

"I really like this car," Isaura told her looking around.

"This is definitely the way to travel," Donna chuckled. "I wonder if she'll want it back."

"I think she will."

"You're probably right, in the meantime let's enjoy it."

Just over an hour later they saw the sign telling them they were entering Ohio.

"The Buckeye State," Isaura commented, "I wonder why it's called that?"

"Because of the Ohio Buck –

eye trees," Donna told her.

"Really?"

"Uh huh." Donna nodded.

Just before noon Isaura mentioned that she was hungry.

"I am too, that last sign said we were only eighteen miles out of Louisville Kentucky, why don' t we find a restaurant there?"

"Ok," Isaura agreed.

Seconds later they were seeing billboards for 'Love's Truck Stop.'

"They have food," Isaura said pointing at the sign.

"I'd be happy going there," Donna replied, "it would save us driving right into Louisville."

A few minutes later they pulled into to the parking lot. There was little doubt it was a hot spot for truckers, there were eighteen wheelers were lined up as far as the eye could see and there were groups of men standing around, as Donna and Isaura drove past a couple of the men turned to sta-re.

"It must be the jag," Donna told her friend with a laugh, "this car is an attention getter."

She found a spot not to far from the entrance to the restaur-ant and carefully pulled in. She would not take any chances, the last thing she wanted was to da-mage Lisa's car in any way.

Hoots and hollers followed the two women all the way into the restaurant and an appreciative whistle from one of four men sitting in a booth near the door caused Isaura to shudder.

"I don't like it here," she whisered moving closer to Donna.

"Just ignore them, bunch of horny old men but they're harmless, god knows how long since they've seen a real woman."

Sliding into the first empty booth they came to, they both picked up the menus.

"With a frown Isaura scoured the laminated paper. "They don't have anything I want to eat," she told her companion.

"It doen't look very appetizing does it? Unfortunately we don't have much choice though."

"What can I getcha?" The waitress asked. She was exactly what you would expect to see in a greasy spoon, frizzy unkempt bleach blond hair, she wore tattered blue jeans and a yellow t-shirt that was grease stained and far to tight for a woman her age.

Pulling a pencil out from behind her ear she scribbled on a pad. "Ya want drinks?" She asked in a gravelly voice that indicated years of heavy smoking.

"I'll have a tea please," Donna replied. "With just milk."

"You?" She asked Isaura with a nod in her direction.

"I'll have a tea too."

"Milk, sugar?"

"Yes please."

"She's not very friendly is she?" Isaura remarked as the woman walked away.

"No, but it probably comes with having to deal with truckers day in and day out, I would think this would be a rough and rowdy place to work, you'd have to develop a thick skin."

She had no sooner said that than a commotion started at the other side of he restaurant.

They turned to look in the direction of the raised voices when a chair went flying, then fists were flying.

"You son of a bitch," one of the men screamed.

"Shut the fuck up both of you," screamed the waitress as she walked over to the two men. The fight stopped and the two men stared at her in surprise.

"No fighting in this place," she continued, "you wanna fight take it outside."

The younger of the two men gave her a threatening look but she stood her ground and he turned and walked out. The other fellow apologized and sat back down.

"See," Donna laughed, "you'd be nasty too if you had to put up with this crap."

Forty minutes later after a surprisingly good meal the two women walked back into the parking lot.

"Another six hours or so and we should be in Atlanta," Donna said as they walked toward the car.

"I don't think so," Isaura yelled, "we're big trouble."

5

"*H*oly shit," Donna screamed running toward the jag. She went weak with relief when she got to the car though, from the entrance to the restaurant it had appeared as if a truck had driven into the side of

Lisa Straub's luxury vehicle, in fact, it was parked at a ninety degree angle with the front end of the truck not quite touching the passenger side door.

"Thank god," she told Isaura heaving a sigh a relief. With her hand over her heart she told her that she'd almost had a heart attack.

"Why on earth would anyone park like this?" Isaura asked.

"That"s a good question. Turning to scan the parking lot Donna cursed. "How in the hell am I going to back out of here?" Walking to toward he back of the truck Isaura told her the owner would probably be back in a minute or so.

"Your probably righ........."
As her voice trailed off Isaura

glanced at her friend. She had gone as white as a sheet and her eyes were as wide as saucers.

"What's wrong?" Isaura asked.

"Does this truck look familiar to you?"

"No, should it?" She asked looking at it a little closer.

"Are you sure?"

"I think so, it di…….." Isaura's hand flew to her mouth and she looked at Donna wide eyed. "Is this that truck from yesterday that was following and pointing at us on the highway?"

"I think so," Donna said running to the back of truck. The license plate confirmed it, it was covered in mud but part of the last letter was visible and looked like a B, and the corner bumper had a dent in it just like the other one.

"This is the same truck," she hissed, "What the hell?" Looking around wildly she told Isaura that they had better get out of this place. "Now! I'm going to back out, you make sure I pull out without scraping the jag."

Jumping into the car she took a deep breath and started the ignition. She was shaking and her heart was pounding so hard she could hear it in her ears. "Just back up slow," she whispered to herself, "and get out of here."

She watched as Isaura waved her backwards, at the same time keeping an eye on the distance between the two vehicles.

"Roll down your window" Isaura told her.

Unable to understand what she

was saying, Donna shook her head indicating she couldn't hear her.

"Roll down the window," Isaura yelled, rolling her wrist in a motion indicating what she wanted.

Reaching for the door Donna looked for the button that would make the window go down. "Shit she cursed, "where in the hell is it?" She hit a couple of different buttons hoping one of them would work. So much for fancy cars she thought, *how in the hell can you find anything with so many gadgets.*

Frustrated she gave up and threw open the door. "What?" She yelled at Isaura.

"You have to turn the wheels that way a bit," she told her pointing to the right of the car, "but jut a little bit, then keep backing out."

Pulling the door shut she put the car back in reverse, turned the tires slightly and slowly inched her way out.

Nodding her encouragement Isaura moved to the front of the car and made a pushing move - ment with her hands.

Seconds later the jag edged just past the front grill of the truck, with a quick turn of the steering wheel Donna drove forward a few feet and waved Isaura to get into the car.

"Let's get out of her," she yelled and began moving before Isaura even had the door shut.

Looking over her shoulder she hit the gas and drove out of the parking lot. "There is something weird going on, I know it was the same truck, it seems like someone is trying to harass us."

For the next two hours they drove in complete silence, both of them thinking about the events over the past two days.

Donna couldn't stop thinking about the green GMC Suburban that had been following them yesterday, and she didn't doubt the vehicles were one and the same.

Her companion was thinking the same thing, remembering the arm that seemed to be waving at them as if in warning.

Both women jumped when the silence was broken by the sound of a phone ringing.

"That's mine, Donna said reaching for her purse. "I don't think I can get it and drive at the same time."

"Let me," Isaura replied. Reaching for the handbag she laughed as she handed the cell to her pal. "Is the sink in there too?"

"Wouldn't fit," Donna giggled as she flipped open the phone and said hello.

"It's Ben," she whispered to Isaura.

"I'm finally heading home," he told her, "but the flight will take me through Atlanta, I was thinking if I planned it right I could be there for the concert and then go on to Toronto."

"Oh Ben, the guys would really love that, what a surprise it will be for them."

"So when is the concert?"

"Tomorrow night, the Georgia

Dome, don't worry about tickets, we'll be backstage."

"Dude that's totally awesome, I can't wait. Where are you staying?"

"The four Seasons Hotel," she told him, "its within walking distance to the stadium."

"Sweet," he replied, "I'll book a room there and we'll hook up before the concert."

"That sounds good Ben, we'll see you tomorrow."

"So he's going to the concert?" Isaura asked.

"Yes, he's going to make a detour on his way home from Iraq."

"It'll be nice to see him again, and the guys will be surprised."

Donna laughed, "won't they? He'll be the last person they"ll be expe..." The phone ringing again interrupted her mid sentence.

"You're popular today," Isaura commented.

Looking at the display she saw Joe Gallello's name. "Hi handome," she said.

"Hey Sweetie, how are you?"

"Good, Isaura and I are on the way to Atalnta to see the last concert."

"Is the tour over already?" he asked.

"Yup, just One Night in Atlanta and it's all over."

"You must be happy that Paul will finally be coming home."

"I am," Donna laughed, "it almost seems like he's been gone forever." When her phone began beeping she warned Joe that the battery was almost dead. "I may lose you."

"I'll let you go then Sweetie"
he told her, "have a good trip,
I'll see you and Paul when you
get back."

Donna had no sooner ended
the call when the phone went
dead.

"So much for this thing," Donna told Isaura waving the phone,
"the battery is dead."

"That was nice of Joe to call,"
Isaura commented. "You must be
really good friends."

"We are," Donna smiled, "I met
him twenty years ago when he
and Paul were in a band together
and we've been friends ever since. I used to have the biggest crush on him," she sighed.

"Really?" Isaura asked.

"Really, Donna laughed. "I use
to take a rose up to him on stage

when the band played."

"And he wasn't interested in you?"

"Nope, he was happily engaged at the time and they eventually married, Paul and I went to their wedding then a few months later Paul proposed to me. Joe and I remained friends throughout the years though, he's one of the nicest men I've ever known.

"I like him too, he is always so polite."

"Joe is a true gentleman," Donna agreed, "he's one in a million."

"So how much longer before we get to Atlanta?"

"About four hours I think, the last sign said it was two hundred and sixty three miles."

Looking at her watch she told Donna that they would get there by seven o'clock. "Just in time to eat."

"Are you thinking about food already?"

"Well I'm not hungry now, but by the time we get there I wi....." She didn't even finish the sente – nce before Donna screamed."Hang on, we're going to hit the ditch."

6

"*L* isa was in her driveway waiting for a tow truck, she had received a call saying they would be there in a few minutes.

"*What a mess* she thought as she walked around the SUV, peering inside the driver side window she shuddered. That Donna and Isaura had not been badly injured or even killed seemed like a miracle.

Thinking she should make sure that there was nothing of value in the vehicle she opened the back door on the driver side, the smell of burnt rubber was overwhelming. Holding her breath she took a quick look and closed the door.

What a stink, she thought. Walking around to the back of the truck she pulled the latch to open the back door, at the same time taking a deep breath, she had no intention of inhaling the toxin fumes again. Realizing there was nothing of value that needed to be removed she slammed the hatch shut.

She was just about to head into the house when the tow truck pulled in behind Donna's SUV.

Poking his head out the window he pointed at the truck and asked if that as the one to be towed.

"Yes it is." Lisa told him.

Jumping out of the truck, he walked over to the vehicle, sniffing the air he asked Lisa if it had caught fire.

Nodding she told him how the flames just popped out from under the hood for no apparent reason.

"Huh!" He said scratching his head. Rocking back and forth on his heels he explained that there was usually some indication that something was wrong before the flames could be seen.

"There was a clunk or something just before they saw the flames shooting up from under the hood.

"Yep," he told her nodding, "sounds 'bout right." Walking to the back of the tow truck he lowered the hydraulic boom, it resembled a long round metal pole that was attached to a large box centered in the back of the truck. It had a sixteen inch chain and a huge hook dangling from the end of it.

"I'd hate to be hanging off that thing," Lisa joked.

"Stand back a bit," he warned her as the boom came down, the chain and hook swinging wildly. In mid air he reached up, then grabbed the hook and lowered the boom the rest of the way so that it was almost touching the ground.

With a grunt he got down on his knees, reached for the hook and crawled under the SUV, he was huffing and puffing and Lisa asked if he was ok.

"Fine," he told her breathlessly, "have to get the hook on the axle properly otherwise it could do a lot of damage."

"We don't want that," Lisa warned him, "or we'd have to sue you."

"K stand back she's comin' up," he told her.

The sound of metal scraping on metal had Lisa alarmed, "what's that?" She asked.

"Nothing," he assured her, "normal sound."

Slowly Donna's SUV began to

raise off the ground, when the back end was the same height as the tow truck he pulled down on a lever and it stopped moving.

"What's that?" Lisa asked pointing to an odd looking box with wires protruding from it.

"Where?"

"Right there," she told him pointing to the right hand corner of the axle close to the tire.

"That's mighty strange," he told her bending down to look at the strange contraption. He tried to reach it but his arm wasn't quite long enough so he got back on his knees and crawled over to it. "What the hell?"

Leaning down Lisa asked him what it was.

"Don't know," he replied, "but

there's a wire running from this box along the drive shaft toward the front of the vehicle. Backing out he stood up and went to the driver side door and yanked it open.

"Oooh, that stinks," he said wrinkling his nose.

"Tell me about it," Lisa laughed, "I already got a wiff of it. Not Pretty!"

Reaching into the vehicle he pulled the latch and walked to the front of the SUV. The heat from the fire had melted the front edges of the hood and he had was having a hard time finding the release.

"Dang thing might not open," he told Lisa, "lotta damage."

"Well I've got tools in the garage, what do you need?"

"'Nothin, I have a crowbar in my truck." Seconds later the hood was opened and they were both peering in.

"See right here?" He told her pulling at the charred remains of some wires nestled in a metal tube.

"Looks like someone wanted this truck to explode, lucky it only caught fire."

"You've got to be kidding me?" Lisa screamed, "this wasn't an accident?"

"Nope, no way." He replied. "I would be wi......" Before he could finish the sentence Lisa was running toward her house.

Someone was trying to kill her friends and she had to warn the two of them. Racing to the telephone she grabbed it off the charger and looked at the directory to find the number, hitting speed dial she prayed she wasn't to late.

She immediately heard a recorded message telling her the customer she was trying to reach was unavailable.

"Damn," she yelled. "Dialing again she waited impatiently for Kirk to answer his cell phone.

"Hello?"

"Somebody is trying to kill Donna and Isaura and I can't get a hold of her I have to go to Atl - anta I have to find them and let them know. The tow truck driver said that the fire wasn't accidental that is was done on purpose we saw an explosive under the hood there were wire......."

"What the hell are you talking

about Lisa? You're talking a mile a minute."

"I'm taking the Solstice and going to Atlanta, I have to let them know that they're in danger."

"Who?"

"Donna and Isaura," she yelled, "aren't you listening to me?" With a loud sigh she told him she was heading out and would call him when she got there.

"Where?" He asked.

Holding the phone out from her ear she glared at it, "are you for freakin' real?" She screamed.

Fifteen minutes later after throwing some clothes into a bag Lisa was backing Kirk's orange 2010 Chevy Solstice convertible out of the garage.

Moments later she was merging onto US-23 S. looking at her watch she realized she was at least ten hours from Atlanta. *I'd better step on* it she thought and watched as the speedometer began to creep up over the speed limit.

At eighty five miles an hour she thought of Kirk and how if he knew she was driving his 'baby' this fast, he'd freak. With a smile she chuckled, *he'll never know* she thought.

The sound of a siren pulled her out of her thoughts and she looked in her rearview mirror, "shit," she yelled. A Michigan State Trooper was pulling her over.

1

"Oooh nooo," Isaura cried.

"Just hang on," Donna told her. "We'll be fine."

As the front end of the car hit the ditch they felt a bump and then heard metal scraping ashphault.

"Jesus," Donna moaned, "Lisa'a Jaguar. The car came to a rest with the front end in the ditch and the back resting at the edge of the road.

"Are you okay?" Donna asked Isaura.

"Nodding she whispered that she was fine.

"You sure don't look it, you're white as a ghost."

"I feel like I'm going to throw up too," Isaura told her.

"Let's get out of the car, you'll feel better."

"You don't want me to be sick in here do you?"

"No I don't," Donna replied, "things are bad enough as it is."

Surveying the car it was easy to see what had happened. The driver side front tire was not only completely flat, there was no rubber left on the rim.

"So that was the sound we heard," Donna said pointing at the rubber that littered the road behind the car. "The rim was scraping along the highway."

"I better get my cell phone and call someone."

"You're phones dead," Isaura reminded her.

Running her hands through her hair Donna sank down to the ground. "Damn it all" she said slapping the ground, "damn....it..... all."

Sitting down beside her Isaura asked what they were going to do. She had tears in her eyes and Donna felt bad for her.

With a brevity she did not feel she gave her friend a hug and assured her everything would be fine. "someone will come along and help us, don't worry."

"I don't think we were meant to go to Atlanta," Isaura replied, "I feel like we're cursed."

The sound of a vehicle appro-aching had both women jumping to their feet and heading to the side of the road. The car didn't stop, it didn't even slow and seconds later was almost out of sight."

"Ahole'" Donna cursed.

"Here comes a truck," Isaura told her excitedly.

As it got closer Donna walk-ed onto the road and began wav-ing her arms.

"Be careful," Isaura yelled, "he might run you over."

"Well I'm not moving so he better stop."

The truck slowed and pulled up just behind the Jaguar.

Out jumped a young fellow wearing a baseball cap and he had a cigarrette hanging half out of his mouth. "You have a problem," he told Donna.

"Ya think?" She replied, annoyed at the tone of his voice.

"S'posed to drive on the road," he told her then began laughing.

"If you're trying to be a comedian I wouldn't give up your day job."

"Don't work," he told her. "But you're funny."

"Haha" she muttered. "Do you think you could make a call and ask someone to come out here and tow us?"

"No job, no phone," he chuckled.

Shaking her head Donna couldn't believe their luck. Looking at the stretch of highway behind them there wasn't a vehicle in sight.

"Tell you what I'll do," he said, "there's a truck stop ten miles up ahead, I'll have them send someone."

"That would be terrific," Donna told him, "thanks."

After he was gone Isaura asked if she really thought he would send someone.

"I hope so, we have no choice but to wait and find out."

Thirty five minutes later a tow truck could be seen approaching from the direction they'd been heading.

"He did send someone," Isaura yelled jumping up and down.

A few seconds later the truck did a quick U-turn and pulled up alongside the road.

"Looks like you've lost a couple tires," he told them as he jumped out of the truck.

"Just one," Donna replied.

"Two," he replied, "both front tires."

Looking at each other the two women followed him into the ditch to look at the front of the jag. Sure enough both tires were gone, the car was sitting on it's rims.

"We thought it was just the passenger side that blew out," Donna told him. Pointing at the bare rim she explained how the car had lost control, how they felt

the thump and heard the rim scraping the road.

"With both of the front tires
gone you're lucky you ended up
in the ditch, if there had been
any other vehicles on the road
you may have been killed.

Isaura shuddered. "I don't feel
very lucky."

Bending down to look at the
flat tire he scratched his head. He
got back up and walked toward
the shreds of rubber that were
scattered along the highway.

Donna and Isaura watched as
he would pick up a piece of tire,
inspect it and then toss it away.

"What's he doing?" Isaura asked.

Shrugging Donna told her she
had no idea.

He finally seemed to find what

he was looking for and
headed back toward toward the
vehicles
and the women, carrying a small
bit of rubber in his hand.

He walked back to the front of
the Jaguar, laid down on his side
beside the tire and began feeling
around the rim.

"What's going on?" Donna asked.

"Just a minute," he told her as
he jumped up and headed to his
tow truck. A couple seconds of
later he was back with a hamm-
mer and screw driver.

What in the hell is wrong?" Donna demanded. "What is going
on?"

"Ah, here it is." Using his tools
he banged then pried at the rim
and a second later stood up.

"This is what caused the tire to deflate he told the women. Opening his hand he showed them a small spike.

"Oh my god," Isaura gasped.

"How did that get stuck in the tire?" Donna asked.

"It didn't," he replied.

"What do you mean?"

Bending down he picked up the piece of rubber that he'd retrieved from twenty yards down the road. "Look at this," he said.

An identical spike was embedded in the shredded hunk of tire .

"That's a real odd coincidence isn't it," Donna asked. "What are the chances of the same kind of spikes in two front tires at the same time."

"About a million to one," he replied, "I think somebody is out to get you two."

8

"Rolling down her window Lisa stuck her head out and called out to the officer as he approached the car.

"Hi" she said, flashing a dazzling smile.

"Ma'am," he replied tipping his hat slightly, "do you realize how fast you were driving?"

Tossing her hair over her shoulder she smiled again, "not really," she replied, "I am wearing my seatbelt though," she told him then stretched out the strap to prove she had it on.

"That's good ma'am, still you were speeding."

"I have an emergency, is that a good reason?"

"What kind of emergency is it ma'am?"

"A couple of friends of mine are in danger, someone is trying to kill them," she explained, "I'm on my way to Atlanta to warn them."

"Really?" He asked, giving her a look that told her he didn't beieve a word she was saying.

"It's true," she told him, "and if my husband finds out I was speeding in his car he'll kill me. Do you want to be responsible for my death?"

He smiled in spite of himself, although he would never admit it he found this lady enchanting, he didn't have the heart to give her a ticket and warned her against speeding. "The next time you will not be so lucky."

"I'll be very careful," Lisa promissed, "thank you sir."

For the next three hours Lisa drove at the speed limit, she was not about to be stopped again, she knew she would be unlikely to avoid a ticket the second time. Not to mention what Kirk would say, he would have a fit for sure.

She was getting a bit hungry but she was not going to stop for a sit down meal, there was no time for that, she would grab something fast at the next rest stop.

Twelve miles down the road she began seeing billboards advertising a "Country Style' restaurant. Just the thought of food got her stomach rumbling and she couldn't wait to get there.

A half hour later she pulled into the parking lot of the 'Sunshine Restaurant.' Taking a look around she doubted the food would be very good, if the way they looked after the property was any indication it would be awful.

Weeds had taken over the parking lot and were sprouting up through the gravel, the building itself was in a state of disrepare, the paint faded and peeling.

It didn't look to busy either, an old pickup was parked in the far corner of the lot and about thirty feet away from it sat an industrial sized dumpster.

By the time she got to the front entrance she was feeling foolish, it was clear the place was closed down, the front door had a large crack in it and there was a notice on the door threatening that trespassers would be prosecuted.

Laughing she told herself what a dummy she was, she should've known just by pulling into the lot that the place was deserted. Her next thought was how far the next restaurant would be. She

had low blood sugar and it wouldn't be long before she would
become lightheaded and shaky.

Pulling out of the parking lot
she turned left and began heading South, *hopefully,* she thought
*there will be some place to get
food, not to far down the road.*

She drove twenty miles more
with nothing in sight and was beginning to feel faint, "dang" she
shouted as she pounded the steering wheel with the palm of her
hand.

Forty minutes later Lisa was
feeling like she might pass out, it
was only a matter of time now, if
she didn't get something into her
system with a few minutes she'd
have to pull over.

Relief washed over her mom –

ents later when she came upon a service station with an attached restaurant. *Thank god.*

She pulled up in front of the gas pump and was met halfway to the front entrance by a freckled young man wearing a baseball cap sideways.

"Hi," he grinned, "what can I getcha?

"Food," Lisa replied.

Giving her a blank look he told her he served gas.

Laughing she told him to fill it up. "I'm just going to run into to the restaurant and grab something to go."

Shaking his head he told her the kitchen was closed. "We only open it for breakfast"

"Are you for freakin' real?" She asked, her voice rising in frusration.

"Fraid so," he replied.

"Ok I'll take a couple of candy bars."

"Don't sell those," he told her, we have gas, oil, and antifreeze, I wouldn't drink them all at once if I was you though." He laughed at his own joke, then asked if she wanted the car filled with super or regular.

"There must be something I can get to eat in there," Lisa insisted. "A sandwich?"

"I'm no cook," he told her twisting his cap. "I just pump gas."

"I'll make it myself."

"I can't let you do that," he replied. Twisting the gas cap off he told he'd be fired if he let her in the kitchen.

Tired of arguing Lisa asked

him how far it would be to another place that sold food.

Looking up to the sky he squi-
nted. "Don't rightly know, maybe
fifty, sixty miles."

"Shut... up" Lisa screamed.

He jumped about two feet off
the ground and stared at her in
horror.

"I'm going to pass out if I do
not get some food, do you want
to be responsible for that?"

His eyes were as big as saucers
as he stared at her in horror.

"Seriously?" He asked.

"Do I look like I'm freakin' kidding?"

"No you don't." Screwing the
cap back on the tank he told her
he'd see what he could find in
the kitchen.

"I'd really appreciate that," Lisa

told him, "I'd be happy with any-thing you can find."

She would live to regret those words. He proudly presented her with seven Paczkies and told her that she didn't even have to pay. "Just take them," he insisted, sh-oving the bag at her.

Twenty minutes later Lisa felt sicker than she ever had in her life. She had eaten six of the jelly filled donuts and there were not sitting well. The shakes were gone, but the sweats had set in and the feeling that she might vomit was overwhelming.

It was no wonder. Lisa was ex-tremely careful about her diet, she didn't eat sweets, rarely ate potatoes and refused red meat. She worked out daily and in fact

a few years ago was into comp-
etitive body building. As a former dance teacher Lisa treated her
body very well, junk food wasn't
in her vocabulary.

Thinking that she might feel better with some fresh air, she stopped quickly to put the top down
before setting off again. Looking
at her watch she estimated that
it would be at least another four
hours to Atlanta.

That thought had no sooner
gone threw her head when the
over whelming urge to vomit
over took her. There was no time
to pull over, she began to heave
and seconds later the contents of
her stomach came up.

At sixty miles miles an hour
in a convertible nothing is about
to land in your lap, as fast as the

vomit came out of Lisa's mouth it whipped past her face.

By the time she got over to the side of the road the heaving had stopped. Pulling down the visor she looked in the mirror and was surprised that there was nothing in her hair.

With a sinking feeling she lean-ed over and turned to look at the back of the car. The black leather upholstery was covered in barf.

9

*D*onna couldn't believe how far behind schedule they were. When they had left Milan early that morning her and Isaura had expected to arrive in Atlanta by about eight or nine that evening, at this rate they weren't go-

ing to be there until at least mid-
night.

The Jaguar had been towed
thirty six miles to a service station and it took almost an hour
for them to put two brand new
front tires on the car. Finally
they were back on I-75 heading
south.

"At least we had something to
eat," Donna told her companion,
"now we can drive with out stopping."

Isaura yawned. "I'm going to
be so happy to get to that hotel
and crawl into bed."

"Me too, Donna replied. "This
isn't fun anymore."

It became even less fun ten minutes later when they were held
up because of an accident.

"I just don't believe this," Donna

muttered in frustration, "it's as if everything that could go wrong is."

There weren't a lot of vehicles ahead of them only five or six, still, they were moving at a snails pace.

"It looks like pretty bad," Isaura said, "there's lot of police cars."

"And two ambulances, I hope nobody was killed."

It appeared as though two vehicles has been involved in a collision, a van and a small car. What remained of the little red Honda was a twisted piece of metal, the windows had been blown out and the roof was crushed in. The front end was nonexistent.

"I don't think anybody would live through that," Isaura sighed.

"You're probably right," Donna

replied as they were waved past the scene by a state trooper wearing a fluorescent orange vest.

"Look there's a sign," Isaura said excitedly. "We're only a hundred and sixty nine miles from Atlanta."

"Only?" Donna asked. "You say that likes it's a good thing.

Isaura shrugged. "I see light at the end of the tunnel."

"Why don't you have a nap?"

"I'd like to but I have to go to the bathroom."

With a groan Donna asked her if she was serious.

"I wouldn't joke about it, I have to go bad."

"Do you want to go at the side of the road or wait for a bathroom?"

"No way I'm going to do it out

there," Isaura told her firmly shaking her head. "I'll wait."

"Are you sure? I don't know how far it'll be."

"I'm certain, I can hold it."

Reaching over Donna turned on the radio, "let's listen to some music for a while. Anything you want to hear?"

"No it doesn't matter to me."

She found a station playing classic rock and began singing along to a Guns'N Roses tune. "Have you ever seen the video to this song?"

"No."

"You should see it, Axel Rose does this dance holding a microphone stand, he's wearing a bandana and it's sooo sexy."

"Really?" Isaura asked. "This

song doesn't sound familiar to me."

"It's one of their biggest hits, it's called 'Sweet Child O'......"

"Watch out," Isaura screamed, as a deer ran across the road no more than twenty feet in front of them.

As Donna hit the brakes she yelled at Isaura to hang on.

The car came to an abrupt stop throwing both women forward, fortunately they were both wearing their seatbelts.

"That was close," Isaura said in a ragged breath, "I thought we were going to hit it."

"I almost wet my pants."

Laughing Isaura told her to go by the side of the road.

"Actually look," pointing to a large billboard she read that in a couple minutes they would be at a rest stop that sold fuel, food and had shower facilities.

"Only three more miles," Isaura read peering out the windshield to read the sign.

"And that'll be our last stop," Donna told her firmly, "until we get to Atlanta, I'll fill up the car there and we should be good to go the rest of the way, I think we're only an hour or so away."

They both ran to the bathroom first, then went into the convenience center to buy a couple of snacks and prepay for the gas.

"Look at this," Isaura called out, "they sell sandwiches, would like one?"

"What kind are they?"

"Egg salad, chicken...um...roast beef."

"I'll take a chicken," Donna told her, "and a chocolate milk."

She paid for the gas and turned to tell Isaura something thinking she was right behind her.

She was nowhere in sight. Donna was annoyed, she wanted to get the hell out of here and back on the road.

"Isaura?" she called out.

"Right here," she replied poking her head out from behind a shelf, "I'm going to get some cookies too."

With a sigh Donna told her she would pump the gas and be waiting for her in the car.

"I'll be there before you're finished," she promised.

"I hope so," Donna muttered. Just as the gas nozzle stopped indicating a full tank she saw

Isaura walking toward her with a large bag.

"We have lots to eat now," she told her with a grin, "let's go."

Finally," Donna replied. Pulling away from the pump she asked Isaura which way was out.

"That way," Isaura told her pointing past Donna to the left. "We came in back there."

"Right," Donna said "and there's the sign pointing to the Inter - state."

She was just about to turn on to the highway when a person walked right in front of the car, if Donna's reflexes had been any slower she probably would have run the person over.

"Is he nuts?" Donna yelled, "I almost hit him."

"Why isn't he moving?" Isaura

asked.

He stood there only for a mo-ment then began walking to the driver side of the car.

"He's spooky looking," Isaura said grabbing Donna's arm.

The person was wearing a de-nim jacket that looked to big and he must have been wearing ano-ther coat under it because the hood of it was out and pulled low over his head.

In the dark with the moonlight shining on him he looked like a grim reaper.

The hair on the back of Donna's neck rose and her skin began to crawl. She glanced at Isaura and noticed her face was as white as chalk.

The 'Grim Reaper' walked up to Donna's window and knocked

on it, both women jumped as her knuckles hit the window.

"It'a woman." Isaura said.

"Yes?" Donna mouthed through the window. She could see her mouth moving but was unable to hear a word.

"Don't unroll the window," Isaura pleaded. "Let's just go."

Good idea," Donna replied and put the gear shift into drive. Just as she was about to take her foot off the brake the woman started to bang her fist on the window.

"Go," Isaura screamed, "go."

Donna stepped on the gas pedal hard and the car raced past the weird woman in the hoodie.

They were out of the parking lot and onto the highway within seconds and would never hear the strange woman as she called out to them that they were in danger and would never make it to Atlanta.

They were the last words she would ever speak. There was no time to say anything when her head was yanked back, and she didn't really feel any pain as the knife sliced across her neck from ear to ear. The last sound she made was a gurgle as she choked to death on her own blood. Silently she slipped to the ground.

10

*L*ooking at the back of the car Lisa couldn't believe it. *Kirk is going to freakin' kill me,* she thought. Opening her purse she desperately hoped she had some wet naps.

"Damn it," she swore, realizizing she only had one tiny package. Using it to wipe her face she decided that at the next service station she would stop and clean up the mess.

She had to admit she felt better, the shakes that she'd had before eating the paczkies were long gone and she assumed that was because before bringing them up some of the sugar had made it in to her blood stream.

Never ever again, she told herself, *I don't care if I starve to death those things are disgusting.* Putting the top back up on the car she put on her signal, checked to make sure there was no body coming and pulled back out onto the highway.

She looked at her watch anxiously hoping against hope that Isaura and Donna were safe and that she'd get there in time to let them know they were in danger. *Who would want to hurt them?* She wondered.

Doing the speed limit she figured she would be there in less than two hours, thinking back to their conversation the previous night she was thankful that Donna had mentioned they were staying at the Four Seasons, as soon as she got to the outskirts of Atlanta she would put on the GPS, it would take her right to the hotel.

She soon passed a sign saying she was only seventy one miles from Atlanta and moments later another that said a service center was just up the road.

I'll stop and go to the bathroom and try to clean up the car she thought, *and if I'm lucky they may have something I can eat.*

As she approached the rest stop two police cars raced past her and turned into the parking lot, from the other direction she was able to see lights flashing, the sound of sirens piercing the air only moments later.

At the same time as she pulled into the lot two fire trucks, two ambulances and another police cruiser entered the far side of the parking lot.

Must be something big she thought, *I wonder if there's been a robbery.* Pulling into a spot as close to the doors of the convenience store as she could get she jumped out of the Solstice and turned to look at the gathering crowd.

The police were pushing people back and putting up yellow
crime scene tape as they barked
orders at the crowd to move.

As curious as she was about
what had happened over there
Lisa knew she had to get back on
the highway as soon as possible,
she didn't have time to join the
growing mob.

Running into the convenience
she store she asked where the
restrooms were, the fellow pointed toward the back and to a hall
next to the milk and pop cooler.

The toilet was a mess and Lisa
was disgusted, she managed to
squat over it to avoid touching
the seat and flushed it using her
foot. She then scrubbed both her
hands with soap and hot water.

As she was looking over her

options for something nutritious to eat she overheard a police off-icer taking a witness statement. From what she could understand there had been a serious crime. With a shudder she moved down the aisle looking for food.

There was nothing on the shel-ves she wanted to eat, it was all processed junk so she went to the cooler on the far side of the store. She was pleasantly surpr-ised to find an assortment of re-dy made salads. "Perfect," she ex-claimed in delight.

She chose a garden salad with a light dressing and two bottles of bottled water then headed back toward the counter, remember-ing she still had to clean the me-ss in the back of the car so she went back to get some for wipes.

Standing only a few feet away was the police officer and a witness. As Lisa tried to decide between paper towels and windex or something ready to use she could hear the cop asking questtions.

"What happened next?" The officer asked.

"I walked out the door," he replied pointing to the front of the store, "and this guy had his back to me and he had his arm around her neck."

"Which arm?"

"Uhm.... it would have been," the young man turned his back to the officer and raised his arm mimmicking what he'd seen, "it would have been his left arm around her neck."

Lisa was transfixed by what she was hearing but didn't want to appear as though she was listening so she moved to the next aisle. The conversation wasn't as clear but she could still make out some of it.

"......you do then?" The Officer asked.

"I ran..........the store."

"The suspect, where................ go?"

Frustrated that she wasn't able to hear the entire conversation Lisa moved to the aisle just behind them.

"....... into a green GMC Suburban."

"How......know.....a Suburban?"

"I'm certain ....a friend ....just like it."

"Did he get into the driver side or passenger?"

Thinking for a moment he told him the passenger side. "The cor.........bumper.......smash........."

Looking at her watch Lisa decided she better get back on the highway, she was wasting precious time listening to the details of this crime.

11

"It was almost fifteen minutes before either Donna or Isaura spoke. Both were thinking about the strange woman that had approached them at the rest stop. It had sent a chill through the both of them, they were afraid but neither wanted to voice their fear.

"Only forty minutes or so to Atanta," Donna told Isaura with a smile, "we're almost there."

Looking at her watch Isaura nodded, "the guys will waiting up for us."

They looked at each other and began laughing, "no way," Donna replied, "they'll be sound asleep."

Moments ago they had both been exhausted, with the journey almost at it's end and the city lights glowing in the distance, they were both wide awake. In a short while they would both be with their husbands after five months apart and both women could hardly wait.

"I'm so excited to see Andy my heart is pounding. "

"I know how you feel," Donna

replied, "I can't believe in a little while I'll be with Paul. I think we should turn the GPS on, it will direct us right to the hotel."

"Do you know how to use it?" Isaura asked.

"No but it can't be much different than the one I own, do you have the address?"

"Yes," Isaura said," it's in my purse." Bending down she reached her handbag that was resting at her feet.

"Hang on," Donna screamed as she grabbed Isaura's shoulder in an effort to prevent her from smashing her head on the dash.

A truck had just passed her, then moved into her lane and hit the brakes, if not for Donna's quick thinking she would have rear ended him.

"What's going on?" Isaura yelled.

"Some asshole driving like an idiot."

Donna followed the vehicle but stayed well back should he decide to slam on his brakes again.

"He's sure driving slow," Isaura remarked.

"Yeah I'm going to pass him." Looking behind her to ensure there was nobody coming Donna put on the signal and pulled out, she passed the truck and was about to pull back in front of him when much to her surprise he sped up passed them on the right and came up along side the passenger door.

"What the......?"

Isaura and Donna both stared at the green GMC Suburban.

"That's the same one from this morning and yesterday isn't it?" Donna whispered.

"Yes," Isaura croaked, "I'm really scared."

As Donna accelerated, so did the driver of the truck. "What in the hell is he doing?" She asked as she tried to keep one eye on the road and watch the truck at the same time.

"He's sticking his hand out the window," Isaura told her.

"Can you see his face?"

"No," Isaura told her, "it's too dark."

They both watched in horror as three fingers curled in and the thumb and index finger formed a gun that was pointed straight at them.

12

"As Isaura screamed Donna floored it and the car shot forward. "Hang on," she yelled, "I'm going to out run him."

"What if he catches us?" Isaura cried.

"I don't think he will, this car

has a lot more guts than the tank he's driving."

" But if he......."

"Stop it," Donna commanded, "he won't be able to keep up with this car."

Unconvinced Isaura turned to watch behind them. She was relieved to see that with every passing second the truck was getting further and further behind.

"We're losing him," she told Donna, the relief evident in her voice.

"At the speed I'm going we may get pulled over by the cops but at this point that may not be a bad thing." She laughed.

Reaching over she turned on the GPS and asked Isaura for the address of the hotel. Once it was entered the voice informed them that they would be at their destination in nine minutes.

"Thank god," Donna said with a deep sigh, "what a trip."

"Hey look," Isaura yelled, poking Donna on the arm, "there's the Georgia Dome."

"It's beautiful at night, just think tomorrow evening we'll be there and our husbands will be on the stage."

"Is this our hotel?" Isaura asked as Donna pulled into the parking lot of the Four Seasons Hotel.

Yup, we're here," Donna told her with a grin, "we made it."

Ten minutes later they were standing at the reception desk both in a state of disbelief.

"What do you mean the band isn't here?" Donna asked.

"They haven't checked in yet," the young lady repeated.

Turning to Isaura Donna told her something was wrong, "they should have been here hours ago."

With tears in her eyes Isaura shook her head, "something has happened to them hasn't it?"

"Donna?"

"Jumping at the sound of someone calling her name Donna turned and saw Lisa Straub walking toward her.

"What on earth are you doing here?"

"I had to come, you have to know that your truck was ri----"

Interrupting her Isaura said "look, there's Lou"

'Lateshifts' tour manager was heading straight toward them.

"Have you heard from Paul?" He asked looking frantic

"No, haven't you?" A chill went up Donna's spine, if anyone were to know where the band was

it would be him.

Shaking his head he told her that the last time he was in contact with the tour bus was late morning yesterday. "I can't reach any of the guys on their cell phones and the bus is nowhere to be found, I've lost all contact. It's as if 'LateShift' has disappeared off the face of the earth."

Book Two

' LateShift'
The disappearance

There was no gleam, no
shadow, for the heavens
too were still. Pale cloud,
no sound or motion in
anything but the dark
river flowed and moaned
like unresting sorrow.

- George Elliot

13

*H*e was in complete darkness when he opened his eyes and it felt like his head was about to explode. He could feel his heart pounding in his tempples and when he tried to sit up he felt nauseous. He slowly laid back down. He had no idea where he was or even how he got here but it was cold, he was laying on concrete and he could smell gas fumes, in the distance he thought he could hear water dripping too.

What about the other guys he thought, *where are they?* It was all coming back to him now, they had done two standing ovations to a sold out crowd at the Housston Astrodome and right after the show they had run out of the building, jumped onto the tour bus and headed to Atlanta. They were on their way to their last show before the tour ended and Donna and Isaura were meetting them in Georgia at the hotel.

He stiffened when he heard a

voice and realized it was Ron, he was moaning and calling out in a barely recognizable whisper but Paul was certain it was him.

Reaching out in the direction of the voice he touched what he assumed was a shoulder, "Ron it's me Paul," he told him.

"Where are we?"

"I don't know" Paul replied. " I have no idea what happened or how we got here."

"Where are Scott and Andy?" Are they here?"

"I guess they are." Calling their names Paul listened for a response and heard nothing but the incessant sound of water dripping.

"There's a strong smell of gas in here, is this a garage or something? Ron asked.

"I don't know, I wish I could see something but it's so dark I can't even see my own hand."

They both stiffened when they heard a sound close by. "Ssh," Paul cautioned, "I can hear something. The two men didn't move a muscle as they listened and waited. A couples of minutes went by with no sound and Paul didn't know if he should be disappointed or relieved.

"I guess it was nothing," Ron whispered. "Maybe it was just a mouse or something."

"It's the or something that has me worr....."

"Owww,.....help me."

"Andy is that you?" Paul called out, relief washing over him.

"I'm hurt," came the reply, "I can't move."

"What part of you?"

"I can't move anything, it's like I'm paralyzed."

14

*P*aul heard Ron's sharp in-take of breath and his own heart started pounding. *Oh my god*, he thought, *what could be wrong with Andy? And where is Scott?*

He felt Ron pulling on his shirt sleeve.

Whispering he told Paul it didn't sound good.

"I know," Paul replied quietly, "I have a really bad feeling." Sitting up slowly he tried to get his bearings but it was pitch black and he couldn't make out a thing, not even Ron and he knew he was right beside him. "I'm afraid to move to far, I don't know what I might hit or fall on."

Ron agreed. "I think we should just stay right where we are."

"You okay Andy?" Paul asked. Other than the dripping water it was silent. "Andy?"

"He must have lost consciousness, maybe that's better." Ron said.

"Hey do you hear that?" Paul yelled excitedly.

"What?"

"Listen!"

The distinctive intermittent high pitched beeping told them a truck was backing up and it was very close to building they were in.

"Hellllllllp," Ron and Paul both called in unison. "Helllllp"

Hopeful Paul got on his knees and began crawling in the direction that he thought the sound was coming from. Feeling his way in front of him he moved across the floor as quickly as possible.

Moving one hand in front of the other he tried to feel his way ahead, with no idea what was in front of him he didn't want to take a chance on hitting anything sharp or otherwise dangerous. At one point his knee hit what felt like a sharp crack in the pavement, "shit," he swore.

Are you ok?" Ron asked sounding concerned.

"Yeah, my knee got stuck in a hole in the concrete, it hurt like hell."

"Be careful."

Rubbing his leg he told Ron he would try. "It's hard when you can't see a damn thing." Moving forward he went a bit slower and using one hand to feel the floor in front of him, he waved the other in a back and forth motion to be sure he didn't run into something.

The beeping sound had stopped but there was a loud bang that sounded like metal hitting metal, then the whine of hydraulics and finally what sounded like stones or gravel being dumped.

"I think the truck is going to leave," Ron told Paul, "he probably dumped his load and that's it."

Afraid he was right, Paul pushed forward a little faster. If the truck was only there to dump it's load then he probably had just a few seconds before it would be leaving.

"Help," he called out, "please somebody help us were in he...."

He didn't finish the sentence but Ron heard Paul's sharp intake of breath and immediately knew there as something wrong. After a few seconds of silence he asked what was going on.

"I... it's....my...."

Ron panicked when he heard

Paul begin to sob. "What's the matter?" He asked. Hearing his friend cry scared the hell out of him and despite how cold he was he began to sweat. He had a sinking feeling that there was something horribly wrong.

"Paul? ....What is it?"

"I don't know, it's either Andy or Scott and...there's....I put my... I think it's blood I put my hand in something sticky and..... it smells like blood. "Ho god, hooo god."

15

*R*on was almost scared to ask. "Is he alive?"

"I don't know," Paul told him. "I can't tell. I don't even know who it is."

"Feel for a pulse or something."

Wiping his hands on his shirt he tried to get some of the blood off then began to feel for either a wrist or neck in order to feel for a pulse – if there was one and he prayed there would be.

"I'm pretty sure it's Scott, Andy has a larger build," he told Ron. He had run his hand from one shoulder to the other and he was certain he was right, Scott had a much smaller frame than their bass player.

"There's an awful lot of blood here Ron, his shirt is soaked and it feels like it's all over the floor too."

"Is he breathing?"

Lowering his head he put his ear next to Scott's face and listened for any sign of breathing, he detected no sound.

I don't think so, I can't hear anything and it doesn't seem as if his chest is moving.

The sound of hydraulics got both of their attention and Paul quickly sat up. With a sudden bang they heard the sound of the truck bed landing back down in it's frame, then the crunch of gravel under the tires as the truck drove away.

That's the end of that," Ron said the sound of defeat evident in his voice. "We'll never get out of here."

"Yes we will," Paul replied, "somebody has to be looking for us, Donna and Isaura will know we're missing and when we don't show up for the concert the police will be involved, they'll find us."

"Oh no, the concert," Ron groaned, "when is it?" Are we to late to do it?"

"I don't know if we've missed it but even if we're to get out of here right now there's no way we would be doing the show."

"Why not?"

"Because," Paul replied as he began to sob, "Scott has no pulse, he's dead."

16

*T*here was complete silence as each man thought about Scott, his two daughters and his wife. They had been married for about thirteen years and with two little girls this was going to be a trage-dy for the family.

Right now they wouldn't even think about what this would do to the band. 'Lateshift' would be the least of their concerns, right now they had to find a way out of this situation and be there to support Scott's wife and family.

Paul heard some shuffling and a small groan from Ron and ask-him what he was doing.

"I'm trying to exercise my legs a bit, hopefully I can get them moving and then stand up."

"Don't hurt yourself," Paul warned. "If you have to stay put it's ok, there isn't anything you can do anyhow."

"I can't just lay here," Ron complained, "I have to get up off this concrete it's killing my back and I'm freezing. I have to help you too, if we don't do something to help ourselves we'll never get out of here."

"It's so dark we can't see a thing, what are we going to do?" Paul asked.

"Why don't I get over to you and then we'll just start moving, we have to hit a wall at some point, we can walk around it until we come to something, there must be a door or other way in here, maybe we can get it open."

Encouraged Paul told him that was a really good idea, "You may be right, we could find a way out."

It hurt like hell to get on his knees but Ron managed it, he had a feeling his left ankle was broken and his head was pounding, but he was determined to get to Paul.

Slowly he began to crawl toward the sound of Paul's voice, it was slow going, every time his left leg touched the floor an excruciating shot of pain shot through what seemed like his entire body. He groaned and Paul asked if he was ok.

"I'll live," he answered. Those words were no sooner out of his mouth when he smacked right in to what he thought was a metal drum. "Fuck," he swore, as he rubbed his forehead.

"What happened?"

"I hit a drum or something." He replied. "My head hurt bad enough before, now I'll have a lump the size of a goose egg."

Paul stifled a laugh, Ron could be very melodramatic and as dire as their situation was right now it was almost a relief to hear Ron being Ron. "Be careful," he told him, "try to feel in front of you as your moving and the concrete too, it hurts like hell if your knee hits a hole. "

"Just keep talking so I can get an idea of where you are."

"Check, check, check," Paul replied, as though he were doing a mic test just before a concert. "Test one two..test...test, bobdolino calling bobdobalino."

Ron chuckled in spite of him – self and thought of their former bandmate Randy, now known as Jackson fox. "Too bad he's not here right now," Ron told Paul, "he'd get us out of here, he'd proobably saw us out or build a scaffold to the ceiling so we could escape through a vent."

Paul laughed. "Yeah I'll bet he would."

A few years ago when "Late-Shift' was a mere bar band Randy Liepsieg was their front man, a talented vocalist and guitar player he also had the knack for building and repairing anything. Circumstances and a move to another city forced him to leave the band before they hit the big time but they still kept in close contact and had fond memories of the years he spent with the band.

"How are you doing Ron?"

"Ok, it's slow going but I'll get to you eventually, the floor is wet here."

"It is?" Paul asked, "is it water?"

"I can't tell, I don't think……."

As his voice trailed off Paul asked what was wrong.

"I think I just found Andy."

"What?" Paul cried.

"I think this is blood, it smells like it there's a lot of it. Andy? are you okay?" He whispered as he shook his arm.

"Ughh," Andy moaned. Ron went weak with relief when he heard Andy's voice and realized he was alive "How are you doing," he asked.

"Where are we?" His voice was weak and hoarse and Ron barely heard him.

"We're in a warehouse or something we think, Paul and ......"

He didn't finish the sentence when Andy let out a blood curtling scream.

17

"What's wrong?" Paul yelled. ...."Ron?"

"I don't know," he called over, "he's freaking out."

Andy was howling now, a loud pitiful sound that raised the hair on the back of Ron's head. He almost sounded like a wounded dog, "Andy," he said as he touched his arm, "what is it?

Silence again.

"Ron?" Paul called, "what's going on over there?"

"I don't know he just started freaking out and now he's gone completely quiet again."

"At least we know he's alive," Paul answered back. "He still is right?"

"Yes he is, his breathing is funny though, it sounds like he's panting heavily. "

Ron turned to move away when he heard Andy whisper something. "He chopped it off."

Leaning down with his ear close to Andy's mouth he asked him what he said.

"It rolled on the floor of the bus."

"What did?" Ron asked.

Silence.

"What's going on?" Paul called over.

"He's saying something but I can't understand and he's quiet again, I think he unconscious. I can't do anything so I'm heading toward you again. Keep making noise so I can hear you."

"Over here Ron, over here, over here." He kept repeating himself over and over shouting loudly and a couple minutes later right beside him he heard Ron telling him to lower his voice.

"You're hurting my ears."

Paul went weak with relief, it was so good to have Ron with

him, he didn't feel so alone now and he was hoping the two of th-em could figure a way out.

After a quick hug they began formulating a plan.

"We have to find a wall," Paul told him, "then we can follow it until we come to a door, there must be one somewhere, we just have to find it."

Ron agreed, "this place must be huge, neither of us have hit a wall or anything."

"It's a warehouse or some-thing, and with the strong smell of gas and hearing that truck ear-lier it obviously isn't abandoned, eventually somebody has to co-me back and we'll be ready, we'll make so much noise they'll have to hear us."

"We better get moving then

there could be somebody back anytime." Ron replied.

Side by side they began crawling along the floor, they waved in front of themselves and felt along the floor before they moved.

After hearing a long sigh from Ron, Paul commented that it was slow going.

Ron nodded, "I can't get over how big this place must be."

"I know," Paul said excitedly, "but we've come to the wall."

"Finally," Ron sighed.

The two of them stood up and stretched, both of them remarking how good it was to be off their knees and no longer in the crouched position.

"Now we have to find a door and get out of here." Ron said.

"Ok, let's follow this wall and

and see where we end up. Do you think we should go seperate ways?"

Shaking his head Ron disagreed. "I think we'd be better off sticking together, this place is so big we might not find each other again, or if something happens at least we'll be together."

"You're right, let's get moving."

Slowly, side by side they moved to the right staying close to the wall, they had both hands raised and felt around as they moved.

"Do you remenber what happened?" Ron asked.

"You mean how we got here?"

"Yeah."

Paul thought a moment before answering, "all I remember is doing the encore, running off the stage and getting on the bus. I woke up here on the floor. What about you?"

"What about that guy? You don't remember him?" Ron asked.

"What are you tal......?" Suddenly it came back to him, "the guy," he yelled excitedly, "on the bus, we asked who he was."

"Yes," Ron nodded, "and he was holding that thermos and he pulled that mask over his face and opened the lid. I don't remember anything after that."

"Me neither," Paul told him, "but he must have brought us here, I bet he's holding the four of us for a rans...."

"........three of us," Ron replied, his stomach clenching as he remembered that Scott was dead not far away.

"I can't believe it," Paul said sadly, "I can't believe it."

"We have to get out of here," Ron told him giving him a push, "lets find a way out."

For the next hour and a half they moved along the wall slowly, feeling for a door a window or anything that might give them a means of escape.

Stopping for a moment to take a rest Paul remarked that either they were far out in the country or there were no windows in the building.

"Why do you think that?" Ron asked.

"Because it's so dark, if there are windows in here there mustn't be any street or city lights, it wouldn't be this dark."

"Your right," Ron agreed, "I've never seen dark like this, even in the middle of the night there's moonlight."

"Oh I've seen dark like this," Paul told him, "in an inside cabin on a cruise ship, just like this you can't see your hand in front of your face."

Ron laughed. "I know, at Ben's wedding, you guys had the fancy balcony stateroom and I took the cheap bottom of the boat budget accomodations, finding the bathroom in the middle of night was nearly impossible, I stubbed my toe every time I got back to the bed."

"You didn't enjoy that cruise did you? Paul asked.

"Too fancy for me, I'd rather be fishing."

"You have to admit the intrigue and drama was rather exciting."

"I'm too old for that kind of excitement," Ron told him, "one minute we were there for a wedding, the next minute it was off, I just wanted to do my duty and go home."

Paul gave a bitter laugh, something about us draws trouble, we were almost blown up by Rick and his crazy brother, Harmon Carter was kidnapped in the Bahamas, Ben's wedding and his crazy uncle almost killing Maria, now this."

"There's a common denominator in all of this." Ron reminded him.

"What's that?"

"Your wife, if it weren't for her we would have been killed when that stage blew up, her, Ben and Isaura found and rescued Harmon Carter, she figured out who was threatening Amy and saved Maria and the wedding...."

She is persistant," Paul agreed, "and when she realizes we're missing she'll do everything in her power to find us."

"I hope Mrs. G can save us this time," Ron replied. " I don't know if tha......."

The same moment Ron stopped talking Paul heard the loud thump and knew that his friend had smashed his head on something. He heard a grunt then a groan and could feel Ron sinking to the concrete floor beside him.

18

*O*ver an hour went by and Paul was frantic. Ron was still unconscious, he had felt his face and body for trauma but there appeared to be no wounds or blood. He did have a pulse, it was strong and steady, still it terrified him that his friend was laying there unresponsive.

   He did know what Ron had walked into, feeling around he had discovered something made of metal and seemed to be suspended from the ceiling. It hung down far enough that Ron would have walked into it, his face taking the direct hit.

   Paul stood there wondering what he should do, he was hesitant to leave Ron but he didn't know how long his friend would be knocked out, he couldn't do anything for him and right now finding a way out of this building was a priority. He decided to leave Ron and go on his own.

   Getting down on his hands and knees Paul began crawling across the floor. Progress was very slow, he would feel the concrete in front of him before moving and wave his hands in front of his face. He was taking no chances that he might crawl into something that could knock him unconscious or worse.

His knees were killing him, the material of his jeans was worn through and he could feel the concrete on his skin, the pain so unbearable that he wanted to stop moving. He knew they were bleeding, but he also new he had to keep going. He was determined to find a way out, he was not going to sit and wait, he had to do something.

From behind him he could hear Andy moaning quietly, he didn't like the sound, at the same time he was relieved, *at least he's alive.*

Thoughts of Scott came back to him and he let out a short sob. *I can't believe this is happening,* he thought.

He felt the skin on his hands breaking down, the fine grit of the concrete was embedded into his fingertips and at the heels and he knew before long they would be raw like his knees.

He was so cold he was shivering, but fear was also causing him to sweat and that was making matters worse, the damp clothing chilled him to the bone.

Paul let out a short scream as he hand touched something furry. He yanked his hand back and rubbed it furiously on his shirt. He was certain it was a dead rat, it was cold and stiff but too big to be a mouse. He was disgusted and scramble off to his right to get away from whatever it was.

Anxious to get away from the dead animal he forgot the importance of going slow and with care. Ten feet later he was unable to catch himself in time, he realized at the last second that he was about to fall into a hole, it wasn't quick enough, before he could move back he went head first into a four foot depresssion, the bottom covered in large chunks of concrete. He felt his left arm snap under him and he screamed as a jagged edge of another punctured his stomach an inch or so from his left kidney. The pain was excruciating but merci- fully everything went black as his head smashed into the floor of the hole.

19

*T*he sound of Paul screaming brought Ron back to consciousness. He lay there for a few
moments, he was disoriented
and for a moment couldn't remember where he was. Slowly it
came back to him.

The last thing he remembered was that he and Paul had been walking along the wall hoping to find a possible way out then the pain, he had walked into something that was hanging in front of him.

He gingerly touched his right cheek and winced, then moved his hand over to his nose, it was swollen and misshapen and he suspected it might be broken. If the pain was any indication, he was certain he was right.

Wondering where Paul was he called out to him, "you here?" Silence. All he could hear was that incessant dripping of water. "Paul?" He called again. Still no - thing. *I hope he's okay,* Ron thought, but he had a bad feeling.

He tried to sit up but the pain

that shot through him was too much and he slowly laid back down. He thought he would rest for a few minutes then try to get up again.

He closed his eyes and was drifting out of consciousness when he heard a sound. His eyes flew open and he listened. "Paul, is that you?" He asked. Another low moan. "Paul?"

From the other side of the building Ron heard the sound again, louder this time, and he realized it was Andy, he wasn't asking for help or even begging for mercy, it sounded like he was pleading for release from the pain, it sounded almost like he was hoping for death.

"Hang in there," Ron called out, "we'll get out here." He heard Andy say no, there was no hope in his voice, it sounded to Ron like acceptance, as though he was expecting a far different outcome, and that it was fine with him.

"We're going to get out of here," Ron called back firmly, "and when we do Isaura will be waiting for you."

There was no response. Ron wondered how long they'd been in this building, it seemed like days, he had no way of knowing. It could have been only a couple of hours but he sensed that it had been much longer. He was starving, he didn't think he'd ever been so cold in all his life and his back was killing him, laying on the cold hard concrete was only adding to his growing list of pains.

He sat up again, slowly this time, and felt a wave of nausea as he sat forward. He took a couple of deep breaths and let the feeling leave before moving any further.

Finally he was able to get on his knees and then he slowly stood up being careful not to hit his head on the same thing that had knocked him out earlier. He couldn't figure out where Paul had gone, the last he remembered he'd been right here beside him.

Hugging the wall he began moving along it again. He knew there was a way out of here, all he had to do was find it. He thought of Scott and his stomach clenched with a sense of loss, he

thought of Andy, he'd already given up, then he thought of Paul,
his closest friend, he was sick with worry about him but he could-
n't stop to think about him now,
he had to find a way to escape,
 for all of them.

From the far side of the building came a new and disturbing
sound, a hard rattling noise. Ron
peered through the darkness his
heart pounding. *What the hell is
that?* He wondered. His heart
began to pound and he froze in
the spot he was standing.

He tried to identify the sound,
a door knob, *no,* he thought, it's
too loud for that. *An entire door
being shaken in it's frame? Yes!*
He wasn't sure if he should be
excited or afraid. He tried to pin-
point the direction of the sound,

it seemed like it was to his left and then ahead, and he judged it was about a hundred feet away.

He moved in that direction as much as he wanted to run to it he didn't dare, he wasn't about to take a chance that he'd fall or hit anything, he would be care - ful, but he was going to find out who or what was making that noise. Ron was convinced it was their salvation.

Halfway to where he was go – ing Ron tripped over a small buc- ket, the pail went clattering away as he hit the floor with a thud. He was fortunate, he went down on his knees first and although it hurt like hell he was thankful at least he didn't break anything in the fall.

The rattling had stopped and

he stared through the darkness in disappointment, he had miss-ed his chance to alert somebody that they were in here. He laid there feeling sorry for himself, al most at the point of tears when he heard the crash.

He quickly rolled over and sta-red at horror toward the back of the building, the noise was so loud he had to cover his ears, it sounded like somebody was try-ing to drive a vehicle through a steel wall.

It stopped. Then almost right behind him he heard banging, he thought he heard muffled voices but knew he was imaging things, then there was the whining sou-nd of metal on metal, and a seco - nd later footsteps up above.

Ron thought he would lose

his mind, Putting his hands over
his ears he began to moan.

20

*H*e was beyond terrified,
he now knew that whoever was
keeping them captive intended
for them to die. There would be
no escape now, it would only be
a few minutes before he and

Andy would be dead, and Paul too if he was still alive.

He didn't have the energy to crawl away, there was no place to hide even if he did, all he was able to do was lay there and wait. Then he heard the screaming.

C'MON YOU ASSHOLE GET THE FUCK UP."

Ron couldn't believe what he was hearing, he was stunned and began to wonder if he was imaging things. He was certain he must be because it didn't seem posible, he recognized that voice.

Book Three

The beginning
Ross and Company

There will come a time when
you will believe everything is
finished.
That will be the beginning.

- Louis L'Amour

21

*I*t was three am and Donna, Isaura, Lou and Lisa were sitting in the lobby of the Four Seasons Hotel trying to figure out what had happened to the band and their tour bus.

Every now and again when the door opened they would all look expectedly at the entrance hoping against hope that the four members of 'LateShift' would come strolling in.

The police had been called but they weren't inclined to do anything before twenty fours had passed, especially since it was a rock band, after all they concluded, it was likely they were off partying somewhere, with drugs and a few groupies.

"We're on our own here," Donna told her three compan-ions, "at least until this time to-morrow, we need to figure out what's going on, the hell with the cops."

Lou agreed. "We know they aren't out having a good time,

they were scheduled to be here, when that bus left after the concert it was driving non stop into Atlanta, the men were excited to be finishing the tour." Lou ran his hands through his hair before continuing, "there's something very wrong."

"Andy would have called me," Isaura told them, "he knew we were going to be here."

Donna nodded, "same with Paul, and if they were held up or there was a problem he would have called." Reaching into her purse she pulled out her cell phone and punched in some numbers, listening for a moment she shook her head. "His phone is still off and that doesn't make sense."

"Why don't I head to Houston,

I'll take the same route the bus should be on and see if I can find them, I'll stop at the rest stops and ask if anybody has seen the bus or the guys."

"That a great idea," Donna told him, "would you keep in touch?"

"Absolutely, I'm going to throw some things in a bag and I'll head out in a few minutes."

As he got up to leave Donna stood also and walked with him to the elevator, "you really think they're in big trouble don't you?" Donna asked.

He looked at her quietly for a moment before answering, then nodded. "I do." He could see the tears forming in her eyes and felt bad, he didn't know what to say, although at this point there wasn't likely anything that was going to make her feel better. "I'm sorry Donna."

She shrugged, "keep in touch."

"Will do," he replied as he stepped into the elevator.

Donna turned and walked back toward her two companions, she felt completely useless and at a loss as to what to do next, her only hope was that Lou would find them on the road.

Movement at the hotel entrance caught her eye and she stared in joy before running toward the door.

22

*B*en was barely inside the hotel when Donna raced up and threw her arms around him. "I'm so happy to see you," she yelled.

Shocked at seeing Donna standing in the lobby of the hotel

he was momentarily at a loss for words. "Dude," he asked with a broad smile,"what are you doing out here in the middle of the night?"

Taking him by the arm she directed him toward the sitting area where Lisa and Isaura were waiting for them. As they walked she quickly filled him in on the band and their disappearance.

Wide eyed he looked at her in horror, "your kidding?" He asked "the bus AND the guys have disaappeared?"

Both Lisa and Isaura stood up as Ben and Donna approached,

"Hi there," Lisa said as she moved to give him a hug, "how's married life?"

"Wonderful," he told her smiling.

"I hear you have a beautiful daughter."

"Yes," he said the pride evident on his face, "she's the love of my life, her and Amy."

"I know what you mean," Lisa replied, "my grand kids are everything."

"You have grandchildren?" Ben asked in mock surprise, "you don't even look old enough to have kids."

"I know!" Lisa replied batting her eyes at him.

They all shared a good laugh and then sat down, reality setting in as they remembered that the band was missing and at the moment they were the only ones who could do anything to find them.

Over an hour later Ben had been filled in on what little they knew about the disappearance of 'LateShift.' Donna and Isaura told him about their bizarre journey to Atlanta, then Lisa told him of her discovery in Donna's truck and how she had come to warn them that they were in danger.

"So this is all related, isn't it?" Ben asked.

Donna's head snapped up and she looked at Ben in alarm. "Related?

"Didn't you think it was?" He asked.

Frowning Donna thought for a moment, "it never even occured to me she admitted, "but now that I think about it......"

"It only makes sense," Ben continued, "I can't believe all this bizarre stuff is random, that can't be, it seems too coincidental to me."

Lisa agreed, "I knew there was something freakin' wrong, that's why I got here as fast as I could."

"Let's walk through this again," Ben suggested, "and see if we can put together the pieces."

It didn't take them long to realize that Ben was right, everything that had happened had to be more than sheer coincidence.

"It makes me wonder how safe you two are," Ben told them. Worry was etched on his face as he looked first at Isaura then Donna.

"I don't think we have much to worry about now," Donna replied, "it's easier to harm someone

when they're out on the highway, but here there are a lot of
people around, it would be risky
for anyone to try anything."

"But not out of the question,"
Ben replied.

Using a couple of Ben's favorite words Donna laughed and
said, "Dude chill, we're fine, I'm
sure as long as we aren't all
alone we'll be fine."

Reaching into his pocket he
told her that might be the case
but to be on the safe side he was
calling in some reinforcement
and help.

Grabbing his arm Donna asked who he was phoning.

" Jim," he replied as he snapped open his phone and began
punching in numbers.

"Pristin?" She asked quickly,

the disapproval evident in her voice.

Ben nodded.

"Please don't call him," Donna begged, "and it's the middle of the night, he shouldn't be awake-ned for this."

Closing his phone he turned to Donna, "Dude, you know Jim would want to help, it doesn't matter what time it is, after what you did for him, for us, he would want to help and you know that, he told you as much."

Ben was referring to his wedding two years before, with a hundred and fifty two guests on a cruise ship along with the band and their wives, it was to be a day nobody would ever forget.

As it turned out the wedding almost didn't happen, during a

complicated and bizarre plot to stop the wedding masterminded by Ben's uncle and his mother, the Pristin maid almost died. If not for Donna and Lisa figuring it all out in the nick of time, Maria would be dead and Ben never would have married jim Pristin's daughter Amy.

"He told you if there was ever anything he could do, remember that?" Ben asked.

Donna nodded her head slowly, "yes but it's the middle of the night and what can he do?"

"With his resources he can do a lot," Ben told her as he flipped open his phone.

A lot was an understatement, Jim Pristin was one of the richest men in Canada and he had unlimited resources, there didn't seem to be anything Jim couldn't do or have arranged.

"Hi Jim," Ben said as he jump-ed up and paced around the lobby.

For the next ten minutes the three women watched as Ben bounced around the lobby, one moment he would stop and look out the window, the next minute he was waving his arms animat-ately.

"Do you think Jim will want to help?" Isaura asked.

Donna nodded, "I'm sure he will, and not just because of the wedding and all that, he and Paul have become good friends."

Lisa frowned, "then why did-nt you want Ben to call him?"

"Because it's the middle of the night and I feel like I'm taking of advantage of his goodwill."

"Well that's just silly," Lisa told her, "he made it clear after the wedding that if you ever needed anything at all to let him know."

"I know, and I re......."

Interrupting them Isaura pointed toward the reception desk and said "here he comes."

Seconds later Ben plopped down on the sofa and threw his legs up on the coffee table. With a satisfied smile he told them that Jim Pristen would be providing them with whatever resources and finances they would require to find the band. "He suggested I throw his name around Ben told them with a laugh, "now that is the kind of power I like."

"Don't get carried away," Donna warned, "power is not always a good thing."

"Isn't that the truth," Lisa replied, "I'm a proud American but look what power did to the Bush administration."

"You can say that again," Donnna told her.

"Look what power did to the Bush administration."

"Giving her a playful push Donna said, "aren't you the witty one?"

"I knowwww, beauty, brains and wit," was her quick reply."

Donna rolled her eyes good-naturedly. "And you know how to own......" The buzzing of a cell phone seemed so out of place that all four of them jumped.

"That's mine!" Donna exclaimed and grabbed for her purse.

"It's Lou she told them excitedly crossing her fingers in a sign of hope. "Hi there, " she said, "have you found them?"

The look on her face went from hope, to disappointment then shock and finally horror. "Your kidding?" She yelled. Remembering she was in the lobby of a fancy hotel she quickly lowered her voice.

Her three companions looked worriedly at her, then at each other.

"That doesn't sound good," Lisa whispered.

Ben shook his head, "no... man I hope it's not real bad."

Beginning to sob Isaura told them she was worried sick, "I'm so afraid something awful has happened to them."

Moving over to the couch to comfort her Lisa put her arm around her shoulders and pulled her close. "Try not to worry," she said. "We don't know anything."

"I know," Isaura sniffed as she wiped tears away with the back of her hand. "I can't help it."

Moments later Donna closed her phone, she looked worried, sad and defeated.

"What?" Lisa asked.

"There was no sign of the bus along the road for two hours, he got to a road side rest stop and pulled in there to ask if anybody had seen the bus, apparently it's now the scene of a murder."

Lisa gasped, then sucked in her breath and all eyes turned to her. "

Looking at her quizzically Donna asked what was wrong.

"I know where that is," she told them, "I stopped there to get some food and the police were questioning everybody. I didn't know anybody was killed."

"A woman in her late twenties or early thirties from what Lou said."

Lisa nodded, "I was standing in the aisle and I heard the cop taking a statement from a guy."

"Really?" Ben asked.

"Yes, the police are looking for somebody driving a green GMC Suburban with a dented in corner on the left front of the truck.

Chills went up Donna's spine and the hair on the back of her neck stood up.

Isaura let a wail then began

to scream.

23

*D*onna went to her and took her in her arms, "ssh, it's ok, it's going to be okay."

"It's the same person," she wailed through tears. "It's the same person that was after us too."

" It sounds like it," Donna told told her, "or a huge coincidence." Ben was leaning over, drumming his fingers on the coffee table in in front of him. He banged a fist then stood up, "ok, let's figure out where we go from here."

"From here?" Isaura asked.

"Sitting here making all these assumtions is not finding "Late - Shift' we have to put a plan toge- ther and take action. If the truck and that murder is related to the disappearance of the bus and the guys then we know what we need to focus on."

"Finding that truck," Donna murmered.

"If we could find out the name of the woman who was killed that might should lead us right to the owner of the truck." Lisa told them.

Excitedly Donna told her that was a brilliant idea.

"Not just a pretty face under all this," Lisa quipped.

"Why don't we do this?" Ben suggested. "We'll delegate each of us a job, there's no use all of us sticking together, we'll each work on an angle independently and see what we come up with."

Donna agreed, "good idea Ben, far more effective and efficient if we're all working on different theories.."

"Right!" Here's what I'm proposing, Lisa could find out who was murdered at that rest stop, she should be the one to do it, after all she was there and over heard some information that might help her find out a name.

"I'm on it," Lisa told him.

Ben continued, "we have to assume that the bus was hijacked or something, it didn't just disappear, so Donna, why don't you talk to the company that owns the bus, inquire, do a check on the driver then talk to the roadies, they'll be at the Georgia Dome in a couple of hours to start setting up gear, it's a twelve hour job."

Donna interrupted him, "two things Ben, this is going to cost money, I know Jim said he'd pay for it but even so, we don't have any right now and I don't want Lisa using her own for any expenses she's going to incur. Furthmore, it's almost impossible to get information with all of the privacy laws in place."

"Ben smiled. "There should be a stack of money in my account," looking at his watch he nodded, "yup it should be there by now."

"What?" Donna asked.

"Jim was putting money in my account to be used for whatever we need, also, we'll be able to get any kind of information we want because hopefully anytime we'll be receiving documents that prove we are licensed private detectives."

"What?" Donna hissed. "Ben we're not."

"Dude chill, it's nothing illegal, as Jim explained to me, anybody can call themselves a PI, you don't need a license, some do yes, but many don't and as

Jim pointed out we've all been involved in solving cases. You and Isaura on Canada Day, the three of us in the Bahamas, you and Lisa at my wedding……."

"So that makes us detectives?"

"According to Jim it does and

we'll be receiving documents any time now, they'll prove that. It will allow us access to inform-amation we couldn't get other-wise."

Lisa shook her head, "he can arrange that in the middle of the night? And putting money into your account too?"

Donna laughed, "when you're Jim Pristin you can make pretty well anything happen."

"Ben agreed. "He wields a lot of power."

"Ok," Donna said, "so Lisa will head back to that rest stop to find out who the dead woman is, I'm going to find out everything I can about the bus driver, what is Isaura going to do?"

"I'll stay here and wait for the guys to show up," she told them. "And when they do I can let you guys know so you can come back."

Donna looked at her friend with pity, she was in denial and would not help with the investigation, to do that she was going to have to admit that the men were in serious trouble, it would be easier for her to wait and do nothing.

"Ok," Ben shrugged trying to hide his disappointment.

"I'm going hook up with Lou

and he and I can talk to the road-
ies and everybody else who was
involved with the last concert, if
anybody can recall anything that
might have been out of the ordinary I want to know."

"That's a very good idea Ben,"
Donna told him admiringly, "you
have good ideas and you're good
at delegating responsibility."

Ben beamed at the complim-
ent. "Thanks dude." He continued, "we should all exchange phone numbers, I'll need Lou's
number from you Donna and I'm
going to run to the bank machine
and get cash for all of us, I hope
our documents arrive soon. I'm
going to ask at the reception for
the nearest bank machine, I'll be
back shortly."

"Well it seems like we have a

good plan of action," Donna told Isaura and Lisa, "I feel a little bit better."

"I don't," Isaura told them.

Getting annoyed Donna told her that sitting around waiting for them to magically appear was foolish.

As Isaura teared up again Donna apologized, "I'm sorry, it's not my intention to worry you but we have to do something other than hope."

'That's right," Lisa agreed, "we have to do whatever we can."

"I'm going for a walk," Isaura told them stiffly.

As she walked toward the entrance to the hotel Lisa turned to Donna, "what's with her?"

"She has never liked getting involved in anything, this time especially would be like admitting that something awful has happened, she'd rather be hopeful and wait than admit to herself that Andy could be in a lot of trouble. Psychologically it's her way of protecting herself from something that is too painful to think about."

"Oh," was Lisa's reply as she shook her head. The look on her face said it all.

"I think I'm going to get something out of the pop machine, do you want anything?"

"A bottle of water if they have it," Lisa replied. "Thanks."

As Donna walked away Lisa spotted a deliveryman walking in with what appeared to be a heavy courier pak. *I wonder if those are our documents.*

Isaura had been walking aimlessly down the street for almost ten minutes, she was crying and cursing her friends. *They're so negative.*

Turning around she decided to head back to the hotel, *I'll bet Andy is there now waiting for me,* with that thought she smiled and picked up her pace.

About a hundred feet from the entrance to the hotel Isaura stopped short, there at the curb was the green GMC Suburban with the smashed in front corner.

Heart pounding Isaura approached the truck. Walking up to the passenger window she cautiously peered in, it was dark and she was having difficulty seeing inside .

A second later the window

moved down and a face grinned out at her.

"Hello stranger!"

The sound that came out of Isaura was nothing more than a gargled scream that nobody else would hear and Isaura could only stare in horror at the face she recognized all to well.

24

*B*en was only able to withdraw two thousand bucks out of his account each day but he thought that would be more than enough, he would split it evenly between the three of them and tomorrow he could get more if need be. He was hoping that by then they would have found the guys and it wouldn't be necessary.

He spotted the women, both standing, Donna with a diet coke and Lisa drinking a bottle of water. They waved excitedly as he walked in.

"What's up dude?" He asked.

"I think the documents might have come," Lisa told him, "a courier was here a few minutes ago."

"Sweet!" He exclaimed over his shoulder as he ran to the front desk.

Seconds later he was back, waving the cardboard envelope. "This is them," he said excitedly. Ripping open the pak he dumped the contents onto the coffee table.

"Holy shit look at this stuff," Donna told them as she picked up a couple of official looking photo identification cards, "laminated and everything," she said marveling at the enginuity, "how in the hell could he get this done so quick and where did he get our pictures? This is photo ID."

"He used pictures from mine and Amy's wedding."

"In the middle of the night?" Donna asked.

"That's Jim," Ben laughed.

Lisa shook her head, "this is un..frea..kin' believable, I'm a licenced PI."

"We all are." Donna said, "and look at this, access codes to the Department of Motor Vehicles, Birth Registrars, we can find cell phone numbers, we have more than what we need, so let's find the guys."

"Right," Lisa said standing up, "I'm on my way back to that rest stop, looking at her watch she told them she should be there within a couple of hours. "I'll call you when I arrive."

"Here," Ben said extending a hand full of cash, "seven hundred dollars, if you need more let me know tomorrow and make sure you keep all the receipts." He gave her a hug and told her good luck.

"Thanks," she told him. Turning to Donna she gave her a hug too, "I'm off to the scene of the crime," she joked, trying to lighten the mood.

"Be careful," Donna warned giving her a hug, "and keep in touch."

"I will," she called over her shoulder as she headed toward the hotel entrance.

"Where did Isaura go?"

Frowning Ben looked around the lobby, "I don't know, she was still here when I left for the bank."

"She must have gone to her room."

Ben nodded, "we can do it without her. I'm going to meet Lou and see what we can dig up."

"And I'll find out everything I can about the tour bus driver. It looks like you gave me the easy job. I get to stay here," Donna told him with a guilty look.

"Dude, don't worry about that,

you're amazing at research and figuring things out, we'll relay information to you and you can decipher it." Handing her a fistful of money he gave her a quick hug and turned to walk away. "Don't forget......"

"I know, keep the reciepts," she laughed.

With a quick smile then a thumbs up he scooted toward the door.

Watching him disappear into the dark street Donna felt sudd-very alone.

Sitting back down she wond-ered where she should begin. *I'll make a list* she thought and rea-ched into her purse for pen and paper.

The sound of sirens made her jump and within seconds there

were flashing lights and a number of emergency vehicles in front of the hotel.

Her and the woman behind the reception desk walked to the large windows overlooking the street.

There were two fire trucks an ambulance, three police cruisers and two more were approaching from the opposite direction.

Opening the door, the Guest Services lady asked the doorman what was going on.

"A murder," he told her pointing down the street, "a lady had her throat slashed."

25

*M*ore concerned about her own problems than those of some woman found dead on the streets of Atlanta Donna sighed and decided to go back to her room. "I'll get more accomplished up there with my computer and a phone," she said out loud.

"Did you say something?" The hotel employee asked.

Talking to myself," Donna told her as she walked away.

The moment she was in her room she turned on her laptop and looked at the short list she had made in the lobby.

First I have to find out the name of the charter company that owned the tour bus, she thought, she had no idea who that was and decided a call to Lou was in order.

Finding his number she hit nine to get an outside line, waiting a second for the dial tone then called Lou's cell. It rang five times before his answering ser - ice came on. "Shit," she cursed, "where the hell could he be? "

Frustrated she told him to call her and hung up.

She sat staring at her computer screen for a moment then got up and walked to the window, at that vantage point she could see the emergency vehicles were still there, flashing lights lit up the street in myriad of colors.

A second later the phone rang and her heart skipped a beat as she ran to grab it. She was hoping against hope that it was Paul and he was going to tell her that they were all safe and sound but deep down she knew it would be Lou.

"Hello?" She asked expectantly.

"Donna hi I'm sorry I missed your call I was getting some gas."

Her heart sank. "No problem Lou, anything?"

"No, nothing. I'm on my way to Houston hopefully if we start from the beginning we can figure this out."

"Ben is on his way"

"I know," Lou replied, "he did call me, he's going to get there before me."

"What? How is that possible?"

"Private jet."

"Oh," Donna replied. She smiled to herself and wondered what it would be like to be the son in law of one of the most powerful men in North America.

"Lou I need some information, what is the name of the charter company that owns the bus?"

"Trans line tours," he told her, "they're based in Toronto. Lee..... he paused, "what the hell is his last name? Lee Som...no, umm..

Lee...Si...Simpson, talk to Lee Simpson."

"That's great Lou thanks, as soon as you and Ben meet up give me a call and let me know."

"Will do Donna, thanks."

Looking at her watch she figured five thirty two am was far to early for Lee Simpson to be at his desk but she had nothing better to do so she sat down in front of her computer and punched in the company name. Reaching for the phone she dialed the number listed.

I'll leave him a voice mail, she thought, *and hopefully he'll call me the moment he gets in, especially if I tell him how urgent this is.* There was no possibility of leaving a message though, the number immediately went to an swering machine that listed the office hours as seven am to eight pm, Monday to Saturday.

"Damn," she cursed as she hung up the phone, "I'll have to wait un........"

A knock at the door stopped her mid sentence.

Paul! She thought with a smile, *who else could it be?*

She raced to the door heart pounding, certain that Paul was going to be standing on the other side with a sheepish grin on his face.

Pulling the door open she was momentarily taken aback by the sight of two police officers standing there, one in uniform the other in street clothes but with a badge around his neck that identified him as a member of the Atlanta Police Department.

A chill went up her spine and she felt faint, immediately knowing that something awful had happened.

"Donna Gardner?" The uniformed officer asked.

"Yes," she replied weakly.

"I'm constable Horan and this is Detective Ramurez, may we come in?"

Fear overtook her and she was unable to speak or think, all she could do was hold onto the door.

"Mrs. Gardner?" He repeated, "may we come in?"

"Yes," she told them as she turned and walked back into her hotel room. "Is this about my husband?"

"Your husband?" He asked looking confused.

"It's not about him?"

"No it's not."

Relief washed over her and she sank into the sofa, "sit down she told them motioning to the two chairs cross from her. "What is this about?"

"I'm afraid I have some bad news," Detective Ramuez told her quietly, "your friend Isaura was found in front of the hotel this evening, she was a victim of foul play."

26

*A*t six twelve am Ben walked

off the Pristin jet and into the Houston Airport. Looking at his watch he figured Lou was still at least a couple of hours away. He was going to get a head start on his investigation though, sitting around waiting for him to arrive was a waste of time and he had to do something.

First he would get something to eat, then he was going to head to the Astrodome. He was hoping somebody there could tell him something that would shed light on the disappearance of the band that had played to a sold out crowd the night before last.

An hour later as he was paying for his meal his cell phone began ringing. *That must be Lou* he thought. Looking at the call display he saw the name of the Four Seasons Hotel flashing. "Hi Donna," he said.

"Hi," Donna sobbed.

"Dude, what's wrong he asked, His first thought was that she had news about Paul and the other three members of 'Late - Shift.'

"I don't know how to tell you this Ben but Isaura has been murdred."

"What?" he screamed.

The couple sitting at the near-nearest table shot him a dirty look and he scrambled out of his seat and headed out the door. He couldn't be believe he had just heard right. "Murdered?" He asked.

"Yes," she told him woodenly, "in front of the hotel a few hours ago, probably while you were still here. Remember we were wondering where she went?"

Running his hands through his hair he said "yeah, I thought she went to her room."

"I had to go to the morgue and identify her."

"Dude seriously?"

"Yes, there was nobody else here to make a positive ID."

"That must have been rough."

"It was, Andy is going to be devastated when he finds out."

"What about the rest of her family?" Ben asked.

"The police are going to notify them."

"Do you think this is related to everything?"

"I'm certain it is," Donna told him, "I can't believe this was some random incident, I told the police about everything that has happened but I don't think they-'re convinced."

"Really?"

"No," scoffing she told him

that they said they would look into all possibilities but it was obvious they were skeptical. "I think they believe she was in the wrong place at the wrong time."

Donna began to cry and Ben didn't know what to say, he was sick about Isaura and knew how she felt but he wanted to be strong. "Let's put all our energy in finding the guys," he told her, "Isaura would want that."

"Yes she would," Donna agreed. "So let's get it done."

"I'm heading over to the Astro dome now, I'll ask around and see what I can come up with, by that time Lou should be here and we'll hook up."

Ok," Donna replied, "I'm going to find out what I can about the bus driver and then I'll talk to the roadies and see if any of them know anything. They'll be shocked to find out they aren't setting up for a concert tonnight."

"We don't know that, don't jump to any conclusions yet" Ben warned.

"Right," Donna agreed rather unconvincingly, "let's plan on a concert. But we had better find them fast if that is going to happen."

"I better get going and see what I can find out."

"I'll keep in touch," Ben told her, "let me know if you come up with anything."

"I will bye."

Ben had no sooner hung up when his phone rang again, this time it was Lou.

"Hey dude, how's it going?" He asked.

"Not good Ben, I was pulled over for speeding and the cops were suspicious, they searched my car and found some crack and heroin. I'm afraid you're on your own because I'm in jail."

27

*L*isa had arrived back at the rest stop to find the place all but deserted. There were a couple of tractor trailers parked in the lot and one car but there was no sign of any people. The yellow crime scene tape was still up and as Lisa walked to the perimeter she could see the chalk outline of where the woman had laid.

She shivered at the sight of it, pulled her coat tight around her then crossed her arms and hugged herself. Glancing around nervously she turned and walked toward the entrance to the store.

"Hi," she said smiling at the sleeping looking clerk. "It looks like something happened out there tonight."

"Yes," he said solemnly, "a woman was killed out there, throat slashed from here to ear " he told her, then pulled his index finger across his neck as if to mimic what might have happened.

"Eeww, how awful!" Lisa exclaimed. "Was she from around

here?"

He shrugged and told her he didn't know.

"Do the cops know her name?

Playing with the tape in the cash register he shrugged again. "I dunno."

"Did she come in here before she was murdered?"

Looking at Lisa suspiciously he asked her why she was asking so many questions.

"Curiosity," she replied. "It's not everyday you see the spot where somebody was murder-ed."

"I don't know anything about it" he told her stiffly, "my shift started after it happened."

"Oh," Lisa replied and tried not to show her diappointment.

"Lady are you here to buy

something or ask questions?"

Not wanting to appear suspicious Lisa told him she wanted
a bottle of water.

"Over there," he told her pointing to the coolers on the left
side of the store.

"Thanks," she replied giving
him one of her widest smiles.

Damn, she thought as she
opened the door to get a bottle
of water, *this isn't going to be as
easy as I thought.*

"Could you tell me where the
police station is?" She asked the
cashier.

"Eyes widening he glared at
her and said, "who are you?"

Putting on her sexiest look she
winked and told him she wasn't
just another pretty face. With
that she turned and walked out

the door.

Getting back in the car she turned her GPS system on and beggan searching for the police staation, *I'll have go to right to the source* she thought. *This should be fun.*

The directions popped up on the small screen and the voice was directing her out of the parking lot when her cell phone rang. "Dang," she shouted. Easing the car to a stop she quickly put it in park and pulled her phone from her handbag.

"Hello?"

"Hi Lisa."

"Hi Donna, any word? Have you found them?"

"No, and I'm afraid I have some really bad news."

"Oh no!" Lisa exclaimed. "How

bad?"

"The worst, Isaura was murd-dered last night in front of the hotel?"

"Are you for friggin' real?" Lisa screamed.

"I'm afraid so," Donna replied, "I had to identify her body, her throat was slashed."

Lisa began to hyperventilate and couldn't speak.

"Slow your breathing down," Donna commanded her, "and breathe through your nose." Giving her a couple of minutes to calm down she finally asked her if she was ok.

"I think so," Lisa replied although her head was spinning and she felt like she might vomit.

"I'm sorry I had to tell you that but I thought you had to know."

"I'm glad you told me," Lisa assured her. "That's so awful."

"I know," Donna told her, "I'm sick about it. "Have you had any luck? do you know anything?"

"I'm at the rest stop now, I wasn't able to learn anything other than her throat was slashed. I'm heading to the police station."

"Please be careful Lisa."

"I will, this is all related isn't it?"

Donna told her she was certain it was. "There are way to many similarities for it to be anything but."

Lisa agreed. "I'll let you know the moment I learn anything."

After they said their goodbyes Lisa sat and collected her thoughts for a moment. She couldn't believe Isaura was dead, it just didn't seem real. Shaking her head she put the car in drive and headed to the police station.

Fifteen minutes later she was sitting in the parking lot trying to figure out how she was going to get the information she needed. She had no experience in undercover work and helping solve a mystery on a cruise ship couldn't constitute PI education.

I'll wing it, she thought, *I'll dazzle them with my beauty.*

Adopting a confident pose she threw her purse over her shoullder, in her hand she carried a note pad, pen and her identification. She was certain that would be the first thing they would ask for.

Lisa quickly walked up the stairs of the tall imposing building and hesitated at the entrance for a moment before opening the door and stepping in.

There was a long counter and behind it a number of glass cubicles but not a police officer in sight. She approached the counter and looked around wondering where everybody was.

"Hello?" She called out. Seconds passed, nothing. "Anybody here?" She called again. Looking at her watch she couldn't believe there was nobody here, it might be a small town, still, the doors were open and the place couldn't be deserted.

Walking over to row of chairs against one wall she sat down, *somebody has to show up event-*

ually she thought, *so I'll wait.* She picked up a magazine and flipped through it. Tiring of it quickly she tossed it back on the table.

"This is nothing but a freakin' waste of time," she swore out loud.

"Can I help you?" A female voice called out.

Lisa was so convinced that she was the only person in the building that the voice made her jump.

"Hi" she said looking at the police woman standing behind the counter. Walking over to her she adopted a look of confidence but friendliness at the same time.

Extending her arm across the counter she offered a handshake, "my name is Lisa Straub and I'm investigating a murder that took place at 'Wheelers Truck and Rest Stop' last evening."

"You're investigating?"

"Yes, on behalf of a client," she offered. The moment it was out of her mouth she wondered if it made any sense.

"Any identification?"

"Yes," Lisa told her timidly. *I hope this works* she thought as she pulled the Id card from her pocket and slid it across the counter.

The officer studied it for a moment, looked up at Lisa, then back at the card and pushed it back toward her. "I can't give you any information on the woman, you'll have to talk to the lead detective on the case."

"And his name is?"

"I'm not sure, let me look."

Lisa waited impatiently as the woman went into a cubicle and appeared to be looking at a file, moments later she was back.

"Detective Collins, he should be here anytime."

"I'll wait for him," Lisa replied and went back to the same chair she had been sitting in. She picked up the same magazine but within a few seconds threw it down and began to pace around the lobby. *Detective work is boring* she told herself. *I should be out shopping for a new pair of shoes.* She smiled to herself as she thought of a pair of Jimmy Choo's she saw the other day. *I'm going to get me those* she thought, *as soon as I get home.*

Walking over to the bank of

windows she looked out to the parking lot and the road beyond, I *hope that detective gets here soon* she thought.

The street had very little traffic and every time she saw a vehicle she hoped it would turn into the station, not one did. "Oh "come on," she said quietly.

She saw a truck coming down the road and slow as it reached the entrance to the parking lot and her heart skipped a beat, that must be him she thought. Turning in the direction she had parked the Solstice the truck stopped for a moment and it was in that second that Lisa recogninized the vehicle and realized what was about to happen.

The driver of the truck gunned the engine then shot forward

and plowed into the side of Kirk Straub's new orange convertible Solstice.

28

*D*onna sat down in front of her computer and brought up her homepage. She typed in Trans Line Charter Bus tours Toronto and the name and address immediately popped up. Picking up the phone she punched in the number. It rang a dozen times without being picked up and no answering machine came on.

"Shit," she swore as she slammed the receiver down.

Waiting another minute she tried again, this time it was answered on the second ring. "Hi, could I speak to a Lee Simpson?" She asked.

"One moment please."

Seconds later she was back telling Donna he was on another call.

"Can I hold?" she asked.

"I don't know how long he's going to be."

"That's fine," Donna said, "I'll hold."

"Ok."

Ten minutes later Donna was

getting fed up, "shit," she cursed, "I could be doing other things." She was about to hang up when the woman came back on the line and told her she would put her call through.

Finally! She thought.

"Lee here," a gruff voice said.

"Hi Lee, my name is Donna Gardner, Lou Reynolds is my contact, he's the tour manager for the band "Late Shift."

"For who?" He asked.

"LateShift, they charted one of your buses for their latest concert tour."

"How do you spell that?" He asked.

"Late ..shift, just like it sounds."

"Could you spell it?

Donna was getting pissed off now, she couldn't believe the guy

was this stupid, pulling the receiver from her ear she stared at it
for a second, shook her head
then loudly began spelling.

"L..A..T as in Tom, E as in even
....shift..S as in Sam, H..I.. F as in
first...T as in Tom."

"You don't have to yell lady, I
got it," he told her. "What do you
want to know?"

"The bus, the band and your
driver are all missing," she told
him, "I'm wondering if you've
heard from him or if you can tell
me anything about him, where
he's from, family....?"

Missing? He yelled, "what the
fuck do you mean he's missing?"

"Just what I said, he the bus
and the band have disappeared."
Silence for a moment then Donna heard a low whistle through

his teeth.

"That explains why his wife is calling here looking for him."

"She has been?" Donna asked.

"When I got in this morning there were a half dozen messages from her."

What is his name Donna inquired.

"Why isn't Lou calling for this information?" He asked suspiciously.

"Because he's in Houston trying to track down leads, thats the last place the bus and the band were seen."

"I see," he replied.

"So can I have his name?" Donna asked.

"What did you say your name was?"

"Oh for Christ sake," Donna swore, "are you for fucking real? Do I have to send the cops over? Are you hiding something?"

"No, no, no," he insisted, "I don't need the police sniffing around this place, what do you want?"

"The drivers name," she screamed, "are you stupid?"

"Calm down lady, I can't just give personal information out to anybody how do I know who you are?"

Donna had had enough and decided to try a new tactic, "you're right she told him, you have no idea who I am and you shouldn't give information to strangers, I'll tell you what, I'm going to send a police officer over, you can give him the drivers name."

Her tactic worked, with a sigh he told her to give him a minute, because he didn't have that information in front of him.

She heard a chair creak, some cursing, what sounded like a file drawer being slammed shut then he was back on the phone.

"Len Stillwell"

"Middle name?" Donna asked.

"James."

"Birth date?"

When he hesitated Donna waned him again that if necessary the cops could get the answers she needed.

" September 22, 1952."

"Where does he live?" She asked.

"Live?"

"Raising her voice again she yelled, "you know, address, his home, where he sleeps at night."

"You're very aggresive," he told her.

"Then you would n't want to see me when I'm pissed off," she warned.

He gave her Brian Stillwell's home address and asked if she needed anything else.

"No thanks," she told him, "if I do I'll call."

"Hey wait a minute lady, what about our bus?"

Donna snorted, "your bus? I couldn't care less about it, I'm worried about the well being of the four men, that were in the bus that was being driven by one of your employees." She went back to her computer and punched the drivers name into the Google tool bar. Nothing came up. Using his birth date she did the same, still nothing.

She tried accessing the Trans Line Charters website but there was nothing to be gleaned from that search either. "Shit," she swore, looking at her watch, she reminded herself she had better head down to the Georgia Dome and let them know there wasn't going to be a concert.

I'll try one more thing first, she thought. Accessing the Department of Motor Vehicles using the code that had been provided with the documents Jim Pristin sent them, she was able to view everything there was to know about Len Stillwell.

His drivers abstract was clean,

going back seven years he did
not have one driving infraction,
no tickets, nothing. From the in –
formation provided there was
nothing that would lead Donna
to believe he could be involved
in the disappearance.

There was a photo of him, the
one that would be on his drivers
license, he was white, bald and
had no distinguishing features
about him other than very thick
black eyebrows.

Shutting down her laptop she
grabbed a coat, purse, and headed to the elevator, she did not
relish telling the powers to be
that there was not going to be a
concert tonight but she knew it
had to be done.

She had no sooner entered
the elevator when her cell phone

began to ring, it must be Lisa or Ben she thought, flipping it open she was stunned to see that it was Paul. "Oh my god," she screamed. I've been so worried about you, where are you?"

A strange voice that sounded nothing like her husband laughed wickedly.

29

*B*en had spoken to four people and none of them could shed any light on what had happened after the band had gotten on the bus. Everything had gone as planned, they had done their encores and then promptly left the stage. From there they had gone directly to their tour bus, drove away fron the Houston AstroDome and from there the trail went cold.

Not sure what to do next he decided to pay Lou a visit at the county jail, as tour manager he would have been there with the guys as they were getting on the bus, he would have been the last person to see them before they departed for Atlanta.

It took him the better part of an hour to get clearance, to go through security and wait for the call that the prisoner was ready. He walked to a long narrow hall with walls made of dingy grey cinder block, he wasn't normally claustrophobic but with that and the antiseptic, institutional smell

he was feeling very uncomfort-
able.

He came to a checkpoint, and
the guard asked him who he was
here to visit then pointed to a
door thirty feet ahead. "Push the
button on the right and step
back," he was told, "it's an aut-
omatic door and you don't want
to be in the way when it opens."

Ben nodded his understanding
and walked briskly to the door,
he wanted to get this over with
and get out of here as soon as he
could, he did not like the place at
all. He punched the button and
moved back as instructed and as
the door swung open it was easy
to see that if you didn't move out
of the way the door would pack a
powerful punch.

As soon as he walked through

he spotted Lou, he was sitting behind a large window, wearing orange overalls that were far to big for him. He seemed to have shrunk and aged since Ben had seen him a few hours ago at the hotel.

He sat down on the small stool across from Lou and picked up the phone, Lou picked up his on the other side.

"I'm surprised to see you here."

"I wish I were anywhere else," Ben replied. "Dude, drugs? What were you thinking?"

Lou shrugged. "I wasn't thinking, you know, you get all caught up........"

Ben shook his head, "no I don't know, I stay away from any of that."

"It's the rock 'n roll lifestyle," Lou replied. "Everybody is into it, it's expected."

Ben gave a short laugh and shook his head, "Dude that's a cop out, not everybody is into it, you're making excuses."

Lou just stared at him through the bullet proof glass before looking down at his feet and shifting uncomfortably on his stool. "You didn't come here to lecture me so what do you want?"

"Information," Ben replied. "I need you to tell me everything you can about the other night."

Lou shrugged. "I don't know what to tell you, nothing out of the ordinary happened, the concert was a huge success, they got on the bus after, we said good-bye see you in Atlanta and they drove away."

"Why didn't you go on the bus with them?"

"I usually don't."

"Usually? So you have in the past?"

"Eyes narrowing Lou glared at Ben. "Are you accusing me of something?"

"I'm trying to find out what happened to my friends."

Lou jumped up off the stool and began pacing around the small area he was enclosed in. The phone was dangling from the short cord it was attached to but still, Ben could hear Lou swearing.

"Fuck this bullshit," he was yelling, "I have enough problems without being accused of having something to do with LateShift's disappearance."

Waving him back to the phone Ben tried to calm him down.

"I'm not accusing you of anything, I'm asking questions, I'm looking for any clues as to what could have happened to guys."

Lou sighed heavily. "Sorry Ben, I'm taking it personally and I shouldn't be, what can I do?"

"I need to know everything you can tell me about the other night, you were the last person to see the guys before they got on the bus and disappeared into thin air."

Running his hands over his face Lou leaned back on the stool. "Fuck Ben, I don't know."

"Let's go over the night once more," Ben suggested. "Did anything unusual happen before or during the concert."

"Nothing that I can think of."

"And after, let's go through what happened after the concert."

Lou thought for a moment then shrugged. "They got on the bus and drove away."

"There was nobody suspicious hanging around, nothing weird happened?" Ben asked.

"Just the usual groupies."

"They have groupies?"

"All rockstars have groupies," Lou replied. "Doesn't matter how old they are."

"I wasn't thinking anything about their age."

"Oh, you looked really surprised."

"Ben shrugged, "not because of their age, I just never thought of 'LateShift' as having groupies."

They all do, look at the Stones."

"That's them." Ben replied.

"It's all bands, look at Ozzy Osbourne, you wouldn't think anybody would want to be with that washed up dick head but he's getting balled every night."

Ben could only stare at Lou, he had no idea how this could be related to the disappearance of 'LateShift.'

"It's all rock n' roll my friend. If you have a hit record you can get laid anytime any place."

Ben was getting annoyed, he didn't feel like Lou was taking any of this seriously and that bothered him. "So there was nothing unusual, there wasn't anything that raised an alarm with you?"

"Other than less sluts than usual, no nothing."

Ben was becoming disgusted with Lou's fixation on the fans that threw themselves at famous people. "So after the concert they went right to the bus?"

"Yes, with the usual bickering."

"What do you mean by bickering?" Ben asked.

Lou shrugged, "Andy told Scott to shut up because he doesn't know when to be quiet, they all get annoyed about that, he goes on and on with no point to his stories."

"Then they got on the bus?"

"Yeah then there was a delay there for a few minutes until the new driver showed up."

Ben's his head snapped up. "NEW DRIVER?"

30

*L*isa has spent well

over an hour with the detective giving her statement, describing the green truck, she told him of their suspicions regarding the murder, the disappearance of 'LateShift' and all of the incidents involving that vehicle.

She had no problem getting the name of the murder victim, she would like to have thought it was her investigative abilities, it was more likely that he was dazzled by her looks and personality. She had complimented him on the shirt he was wearing and told him he didn't look like a detective but more as a male model. He blushed and waved her off but it was easy to see he was taken with her. Pulling out the murder book he had shared all the information he knew as Lisa jotted everything down on her writing pad.

An hour later she was walking down the stairs to the waiting taxi, she was heading to a rental company to get a car and would head back to Atlanta. She had no sooner given the driver directions when her phone began ringing.

"Hi Ben," she said putting the cell to her ear.

It took her ten minutes to tell him everything that had happened, he couldn't believe it when she told him that the truck was brazen enough to smash the Solstice in the parking lot of the police station.

"Your in danger," he warned, "they know who you are so be very careful."

"I will," she promised. "I won't be taking any chances."

"Have you learned anything?" She asked.

"Yeah, their bus driver was

switched at the last minute so whoever replaced him was likely in on the disappearance."

"Lisa whistled, "the dots are starting to connect."

Ben agreed. "Once we have all the pieces of the puzzle we'll have the guys back. So were you able to find out the name of the woman who was murdered?"

"Yes I did," Lisa told him proudly, "I was able to find out everything about her.

"Good for you, see you make a good PI."

Lisa beamed. "Her name was Karen Oleswky, she's from Oshawa, Ontario.

"Oshawa?" Ben asked. He was surprised, that was the last thing he expected to hear.

"There's more," Lisa told him,

"you won't believe this but they found a ticket stub in her purse, she was at the 'LateShift concert the other night."

31

*D*onna was still reeling after hearing the voice coming from Paul's phone. If there was any doubt before it was gone now, it was clear that the men had been snatched, bus and all and whoever was behind this had Paul's cell phone.

Her phone began to ring as she got stepped off the elevator but she decided to ignore it, the last thing she wanted was to hear that voice again.

She walked through the lobby heading for the parking lot when the phone began ringing again, still she ignored it, she had no intention of answering. It continued to ring while she made arrangements to rent an SUV, as much as she had enjoyed driving Lisa's jaguar she wasn't about to take any more chances that it could be damaged, she thought it best to leave it parked safely and arrange for a rental. Finally fed up with her cell, Donna reached into her purse to shut it off. As she hit the settings button she realized it was Ben's name flashing. She was too late though, by the time she answered he was gone. Waiting until she had located the white Lexus RX10, she jumped in then quickly called Ben back. "Sorry," she apologized when he said hello.

He was stunned when she told him about the call from Paul's phone and then he told her what had happened to Lisa.

"Oh my god Ben, these people are so brazen."

"I know, its like they aren't afraid of anything, and that makes them even more dangerous."

Donna agreed, "the guys are in a lot of danger. Where do we go from here?"

Ben thought for a moment, "I think you should let them know

that there won't be a concert tonight."

"I'm heading there now."

"Ok, Lisa is on her way to Oshawa, she's going to find out ever-
rything she can about Karen, the
woman who was murdered. "I'm
going to head back there, hopefully by the time I get back we'll
have some new leads to work
on."

Donna began crying, "I'm so
glad you're coming back Ben, it
will be good to have you here."

Ben didn't know what to say
to comfort her, his best friend,
her husband was missing and he
felt helpless. "Dude, we'll find the
guys, I promise."

Pulling out of the underground
parking lot Donna had to shield
her eyes from the bright sun, "I

know, there's just so many things happ......" She didn't finish the
sentence, instead she let out an
ear piercing scream.

"Donna what's wrong?" Ben
yelled.

It's a....oh my.. god....I...a....."

"Donna what is it?

"A ...oh...some....oh Ben....."
She began to scream.

"Its...I don't know...I think.. "
She began to hyperventilate.

"Donna breathe slowly," Ben
commanded. He waited a minute
for her to calm down then asked
her what was wrong.

"Oh god," she moaned, "somebody's head just fell on my windshield."

32

*L*isa was only a few min-

utes from landing at the Municipal Airport in Oshawa, Ontario. Ben had instructed her to find out everything there was to know about Karen Olewsky, he wanted to know who she was, why she would be in Atlanta, and most importantly what she may have been involved in that would cause her to end up dead.

She was on a Pristin private jet, one of two in the fleet. It was a Gulfsream G550, a nine seat plane that had every conceivable luxury. The interior was finished in a soft cream colored leather, the dining room sat ten, it had a bedroom, two luxurious bathrooms, the bar was fully stocked and Lisa was enjoying her second Mimosa. She had already eaten, she was served the freshest sushi she had ever tasted.

I could get used to traveling like this, she thought. There were two cabin stewards, both couldn't do enough for her, one offered magazines, the other was serving drinks and food. She was just finishing her drink when the head steward came over and re-moved the glass out of her hand.

"We're about to land," he informed her.

An hour later Lisa had cleared Canadian customs and was gett-ting into her rental car. She set the GPS system and was head-ng to the last known address of the rest stop murder victim.

It was early morning and there was a lot of traffic, still, she rea-ched her destination in less than ten minutes. It wasn't the nicest neighborhood, the row houses were run down, many of the por-ches had accumulated junk on them, there were bicycle parts

scattered about, a bag of garb-
age was at the curb and looked
as if it had been torn into, probably by birds. Its was spilling out
onto the sidewalk and Lisa could
see clusters of maggots as she
walked by. She covered her nose
and gagged, the smell coming from that bag was disgusting, like
rotting meat.

Dodging toys and old bike parts
she made her way up the steps
to the the door, the covered por-
ch was a mess, there were blank-
kets tossed in a corner and a big
old orange cat was sleeping on
top, an artificial Christmas tree
decorations and all had been tossed out and was now laying
on it's side in the corner, a couple of what looked liked used
baby diapers were laying beside

the door, beside them a potted plant, now dead, the foliage yellow and shrivelled.

Neglect was everwhere and Lisa felt depressed just standing there. She hesitated, then rapped sharply on the door. Inside she could hear a baby screaming and a tv was on, it was turned up so loud she was able to identify the voice of Big Bird, they were watching Sesame Street.

Nobody came to the door, so she rapped again, louder this time. Still no answer. *They probably can't hear over the racket in there*, she thought. She glanced around nervously, the neighborhood made her uneasy and she wanted to find out what she neeed to then get the hell out here.

She was about to knock again

when a voice from behind asked her what she wanted. She jumped, then swiveled around to see a young black woman standing at the top of the stairs. She looked to be in her late teens, she could have been attractive but her hair was dirty and unkempt, she was wearing a striped bikini top and jeans that sat low on her hips, far below her navel and much lower than what could be considered decent.

Flashing her a bright friendly smile Lisa said hi. The girl looked at her suspiciously. *In this area someone can't be too careful* Lisa thought, *and looking like I do she knows I'm not from around here. She's probably isn't used to gorgeeous women in designer clothing showing up on her doorstep.*

"Whadda ya want?

"I'm trying to find out about a woman that lived here," Lisa told her.

"Who?" She asked as she pushed past Lisa and unlocked the door. She walked in then turned and asked Lisa if she was coming in.

The smell assaulted Lisa, anderlying scent of urine, bacon grease, dirty clothes and mold, it was all she could do not to gag.

The baby was standing in a playpen and stopped screaming the moment she saw the girl, she reached out her arms to be picked up and began babbling excitcitedly.

"Wasn't there anybody here with her?" Lisa asked, her eyes wide with shock.

"Hadta get smokes," the girl said defensively, "she's ok, door was locked." Her eyes narrowed. "You from child welfare?"

"No," Lisa assured here, "I'm here to find out about a woman who lived at this address."

"You sure? Are you lyin' to me?"

Lisa had a feeling that unless she could gain this girls trust she woudn't be getting any information.

Winking at the girl Lisa asked her if she had ever met anyone from social services who had ever dressed this well.

"You gotta point there," she replied, "those skags don't look like you." Grinning she commented on Lisa'a shoes.

"They're Jimmy Choo's."

"Sweet, maybe someday I'll get me a pair of them things."

"I bet you will," Lisa told her.

"So who'd ya want to ask me about?"

Lisa removed the picture of Karen from her purse and set it on the table, "do you recognize this woman?"

She looked at it and said "ya that's my roommate Karen Olew-sky. She in trouble?"

Lisa braced herself for what was about to come then told her she was the victim of foul play. She couldn't believe it when the girl started laughing. *Shock,* Lisa thought.

"What'd ya say your name was?" She asked.

"Lisa."

"Whatta you got ta do wiff

Karen?"

"I'm investigating her death and I'm hoping you can tell me something that might help me find out who would want her dead."

She shrugged. "I dunno, mostly she kept to herself."

Did she have a boyfriend?"

"Ya, a fuckin loser. Treated her like shit."

"What was his name?"

She shrugged again, "I don't remember, she called him her man." Jumping up she went over to the fridge and pulled a picture out from under a magnet. "This is him."

Looking at the picture Lisa commented that he was a good looking guy. "When was this picture taken?"

"Bout a month ago, right here sittin' at this table."

Lisa looked at the picture and nodded, "they looked happy."

The girl scoffed. "They was happy s'long as she did what he wanted."

"He was abusive?"

"He was a fuckin' a-hole."

"When did you see her last?"

"Last week, she said, "they was going on road trip."

"Where too?"

"I dunno, the states is all I's told."

"Did they fly?"

The girl chuckled, "fly? They had no pot to piss in, they went in his truck."

"What kind of truck does he drive?"

"I dunno what it is, an old beat up green truck is all."

33

*B*en had to find out who had replaced Len Stillwell as the bus driver. If he could figure that out he was almost certain it was going to lead him right to 'Late - Shift.'

After Donna had screamed

that there was a head on her windshield Ben had instructed her
to call 911 immediately then
waited for her to call him back.
She did moments later and he
stayed on the phone with her
until the police arrived. He was
still shaken and he couldn't imagine what Donna was going though having seen that. *She must
be traumatized,* he thought.

He was on his way back to the
Houston Astrodome, he desperately hoped somebody could tell
him something about the fellow
who had replaced the bus driver
at the last minute, *somebody
must have seen something* he
thought and he wanted to talk to
the person who had allowed him
into a secure area.

Thirty minutes later after being stuck in a traffic jam caused by road construction Ben arrived and was looking for a parking spot. *So Toronto isn't the only city that does all their roadwork during peak traffic.*

He pulled into a spot not far from the building, grabbed his identication and headed toward the building. He felt a sense of sadness when he thought that it was in this place that his friends were last seen, they had played to a sold out crowd then left the building looking forward to doing one more concert before heading home. Ben shook his head, *What could have happenened?* He wondered.

He was quickly stopped by security as he attempted to enter the building and he couldn't help but wonder how a person other than Len Stillwell was able to gain access.

Removing his identification, he showed the guard and explained he was here to investigate the disappearance of 'LateShift.'

The security guy didn't even look at the card Ben was holding out to him, he looked shocked.

"LateShift,' from the concert here the other night?"

Ben nodded.

"Are you shittin' me?" He asked.

"I'm afraid not," Ben replied, "they got on their tour bus and haven't been seen since."

"I was right there when they got on the bus," he told Ben, "all seemed well."

"Dude seriously? You were

there?"

"Sure was. I move around, sometimes I'm up here, if there's a baseball game I'm out near the stands, if there's a concert I'm down there making sure nobody but authorized personell get any where near the bus or the band."

Ben couldn't believe his good luck. "Well somebody did get to them, it looks like bus drivers were switched at the last minute. do you no anything about that?"

"No nothing. By the way the name's Wade, Wade Kimball."

"Nice to meet you Wade," Ben said as they shook hands, "look could I ask you a few questions?"

"Yeah sure," he said nodding, "anything I can do to help."

"Somehow a new bus driver was substituted, any idea how

that could happen?"

Wade thought for a moment, "I know it was a different driver, he said he was a replacement."

"Did he not have to show proof of that? Was he taken at his word and allowed on the bus?"

"No no," Wade replied, "shit it wasn't like that, he showed the papers from the bus company saying he was their driver, since the other guy wasn't here there was no need to question him. I'm careful about things like that," he added quickly, "I don't like to take chances."

Ben looked at him skeptically, "dude, you didn't even look at my identication, you have no idea who I am but you're answering my questions."

Wade looked at his feet and

shuffled uncomfortably, "are you going to get me fired?"

"No, I just want answers."

"What can I tell you?"

"The replacement driver I want to know everything about him."

Wade scrached his arm, "not much to tell, the guy pulls in, he comes over and says he's the new driver because the other is sick. He shows me his license and the papers from the charter company and gets on the bus."

"Did you take a good luck at the papers? Do you know his name?"

Wade shifted uncomfortably.

Ben raised his voice. "Did you get his name?"

"No," he whispered.

"I can't hear you," Ben practically shouted, "did you bother

checking out his papers or looking at his licence?"

Wade shook his head. "No I
didn't."

Ben stared at him. "What
can you tell me about the guy?"

"He was tall and had dark
hair."

"That's all," Ben asked? "Any
tattoos?"

"Not that I could see, he was
wearing a jacket."

"Any scars, anything about
him that would stand out?"

Wade shook his head slowly,
"no, nothing I can thing of."

"And you didn't get his...."

"Wait," he interrupted, "he had
an earing in his ear."

"What kind of earing?" Ben
asked.

"A diamond stud."

"Other than that there was nothing about him?"

"No, he was like any other guy normal, everyday."

"Ok," Ben told him. "I'm going to leave you my number and if you think of anything give me a call."

" I can do that," Wade replied, "do you want me to call you when he comes back for his truck?"

Ben almost fell over. "His truck is here?" He croaked.

"Yeah, it's right where he parked it. Fifty feet from where the tour bus was sitting."

"I need to get into it," Ben told him. "I need your help Wade."

"I can't do that, I could lose my job."

"You could lose your job if anybody finds out that you weren't doing your duty the other night."

"So this is blackmail?"

Ben chuckled, "no, let's call it incentive, you help me out and nobody has to know anything about the other night."

Wade stood there looking at Ben, he seemed to be weighing his options.

"Tell you what I'll do," Ben said agreeably, "you don't have to do anything illegal, just stand watch while I get into the truck."

Wade looked both scared and unconvinced that he wasn't going to land in a heap of trouble.

"You have a choice Wade, help me out and hope for the best or lose your job when I tell your boss that you're responsible for the disappearance of 'Late Shift.'"

"This way," he told Ben stepping through the doors and into the Astrodome.

It took more than twenty minutes to make their way to the back lot behind the dome. Four sets of escalators, security doors, they had to pass through an xray mchine, up a flight of stairs, and finally down a narrow hallway before emerging in a large open area with a bank of windows on the far side.

"Their dressing rooms were right over there," Wade told Ben as he pointed to the left, "then they came out here and went through those doors and got on the bus, the truck that guy drove is right out there."

They walked outside and Ben

followed Wade toward a late model white Toyota Tacoma.

"This is it?"

"Ben peered in the window then tried the door, it was lock - ed. "Crappers, I guess it would have been too easy to just open the door, I'll have to break in."

"Whoa, no way!" Wade practically shouted. Looking around frantically he told Ben he could- n't let him break into the truck.

"Turn your head then," Ben replied, "and let me know if you see anybody coming." He hoped everything he'd ever seen on tv would work, he braced himself next to the truck, bent his arm, and using all of his weight sma- shed his elbow into the drivers side window. The first thought to go through Ben's mind was that you should never believe what you see on TV, the second was that he might pee his pants. Then his face went white, his entire body began to shake then he slowly fell to the ground. He had never known pain like this, it radiated from his elbow, down his arm and seemed to encompass his entire body.

"Hey, you ok?" Chad asked kneeling down beside him.

Ben groaned in agony.

"Is there anything I can do for you?"

"Do you have a gun?"

"No," Wade replied in horror, "why?"

"Because," Ben croaked "I was hoping you could shoot me."

Chad heaved a sigh of relief.

"Can you get me a coat hanger?"

"Huh? What for?"

"I have to get into that truck."

Wade stared at him wide ey-ed."Are you for real?"

"Of course I am."

Wade told him he was crazy, "look buddy I'd like to help but I can't break into the truck, that's illegal, I could end up in jail."

"I'm the one doing the break-ing in," Ben replied. "you'll be the lookout, that's not illegal."

"That's an accomplice."

"That's on tv, trust me not everything you see on tv is true."

Wade laughed, I'm not that stupid pal, if I let you break into that truck I'm as guilty as you."

Ben gave a frustrated sigh.

An hour and a half later he was on his way to the airport. It had taken plenty of convincing but somehow he had manage to get Wade to find him a coat hanger and look the other way as Ben jimmied his way into the truck. Luck was with him and he found the insurance certificate vehicle registration and insurance in the glove compartment.

He had called Donna with the information and told her he'd see her at the hotel within a couple of hours, meantime she was going to do a search and find out what she could. There was little doubt that if they could locate the driver of that truck he would lead them to 'LateShift.'

34

*T*en thirty am. Donna had be-
en awake for twenty eight hours
straight and she was feeling it,
her brain was fuzzy and she was
shaky, she hadn't eaten anything
either and the toll on her body
was beginning to show. She did-

nt care, her only thought was to find her husband and his band, once that was done she would eat and sleep.

Both Lisa and Ben were on their way back to Atlanta, they each had information that they thought would lead them to the band. While she was waiting for them she would be doing a search on a couple of names that Ben had provided.

First she needed something to drink, something to help wake her up. She walked down the hall to the pop machine, put a dollar bill in and punched the button to get a diet coke. She popped the tab and drank half the can before she was back in her room.

She laughed at the lecture she would get from Lisa for drinking the stuff, a self confessed health and fitness nut, she would be quick to remind Donna that the aspartame was bad for her. She hoped her friends arrived back soon, she'd gladly suffer through lectures about her eating habits if it meant having the company of both Lisa and Ben.

It had been an awful morning, she had almost passed out when the head had fallen on her windshield and if it hadn't been for Ben on the other end of the phone line she surely would have. He was calm and kept her that way, he instructed her to call the police then stayed on the phone with her until they arrived. It was his calm, quiet demenour that kept her sane.

She gave the police her state-

ment and watched as they bag-
ged and tagged the head then
searched for other evidence, she
reminded them that 'LateShift'
was missing, still, they refused to
launch any kind of search until at
least twenty four hours had gone
by and they made it clear that
they didn't believe that a link ex-
isted. Donna couldn't believe it.
Adding insult to injury the lead
detective asked her not to leave
town saying he may have further
questions and wanted her to be
available until the case was reso-
lved to his satisfaction. She knew
he couldn't demand she stay and
under any other circumstances
she would have told him how
to go screw himself, but until the
band was found she was staying
right here. While she was wait-

ing for Ben and Lisa to arrive she would see what she could dig up with the information Ben had provided.

Sitting down in front of her laptop she brought up the Google homepage and began a search. According to Ben he had located the truck that was driven by the fellow he believed somehow managed to replace Len Stillwell as the tour bus driver.

Looking at the writing pad she could barely read what she had scratched out during her call with Ben. There were two names, it appeared as though the vehicle was insured to a K. Eldridge Connstruction Ltd, the ownership in the name of a Jim Reigns.

Chewing on the inside of her cheek, she stared at the names,

something about it looked famil-
liqar, there was something twig-
ging at her brain, it wasn't com-
ming to her though, fatigue made
her brain foggy and she was not
thinking clearly.

She typed in the name of the
construction company with
Houston behind it and hit enter,
the closest thing to pop up was
Eldridge Contracting. *Crap!* She
thought.

She tried again, elimimating
the K. Same results. "Fuck!" she
swore out loud. *There must be
something here.* She stared at
the screen wondering what to
try next. *I wonder,* she thought
and typed in only the word con-
tactors. Up popped a listing for
dozens of companies in the grea-
ter Houston area, she scrolled

down to the e's hoping to see the name, again it was not there. She wondered if it was possible it hadn't made in online, she did find that highly unlikely but on the off chance that was a possibility she went the drawer in the night table beside the bed to get the phone book. It wasn't there, going to the other side of the bed she was disappointed to find that it was empty too. She looked around the room and wondered if perhaps there wasn't one here. *No! There has to be,* she thought.

She looked at the armoir that that the tv was in, it had three drawers in the bottom, opening the first one she was pleased to see two books, one for white pages the other for yellow. She reached in and scooped up both. Quickly sooping them up she went back to the desk and flipped open the yellow book and went to contractors. Running her fingers down the list she was surprised to find nothing by the name of Eldridge. "Damn it all", she cursed.

She tossed the book aside and opened the white pages, finding the e section again she found the name, there were three of them, picking up the phone she dialed the first number, an elderly woman said hello on the first ring, "hi" Donna said, "I'm trying to reach Eldridge contracting,"

"There's nobody here by that name," the woman told her.

"Ok thank you."

Donna dialed the next number. It only rang once and a cheery voice came on the line saying her and Rod were at the Watkins convention and would be back a week Tuesday, she went on to tell the caller that if you had an order you could leave it after the beep.

She called the last number, it rang seven times and she was about to hang up when a young child answered the phone.

"Can I talk to your mommy?" Donna asked.

"Mommy go esway sto, go by keppy."

"Oh," Donna told him, "can I talk to somebody else?"

"Mommy home back esway."

Donna was getting frustrated. "Is there somebody else I can...?"

"Hello a teenage voice said breathlessy.

"Hi," Donna said with relief.

"Hi backatcha,"

"I'm looking for a company by the name of Eldridge Contractors. "

"Oh, well there's no company by that name here. Jason works for BP and Trish is a hairdresser."

"Have you ever heard of that company?" Donna asked.

"No," she said. "Doesn't sound familiar."

"Thanks, bye." Donna hung up. She was perplexed, she couldn't understand how any company could be listed on an insurance certificate but not appear to be in existance. Opening the white pages again she looked for the name Jim Reigns, there was not one listing under that name. *This*

doesn't make sense she told herself, *it can't be.*

Bringing up the google homepage she decided to try something else, wondering if she was
being too specific about the loca-
tion she tyed in address and phone numbers and up popped half
a dozen websites, she clicked on
the first one, checked the spell
lling of Jim Reigns then typed in
the name. Two seconds later she
found out there were two hundred and twenty one results for
the entire country. With a sigh
she began looking through the
names for addresses that would
fit the criteria for further investigation, she was willing to
consider anything in Texas and
elimate anything out of the state.

The first twenty six were from Missour, Florida, New Jers-
ey......By the time she was over a
hunded and ten she had elimina-
d names in Ohio, Nevada, Delaw-
are, Washington, "fuckin jesus,"
she swore.
Donna couldn't believe it, Lisa
and Ben woud be back anytime
and she had nothing.

She sat back for a moment,
then leaned forward and scrolled the list some more. Mississipi
was on the list, Vermont, Tenne-
ssee....ten minutes later she saw
the name jim Reigns in Georgia.
She passed that one and kept going down the list. A minute later
she stopped, she when back up
and stared at a name that was
located in a place named Druid
Park. She stared at it. *I wond-*

er, with her heart pounding she brought up MapQuest and typed in directions from Atlanta to Drid Park. Moments later she sucked in her breath, the driving time popped up as eleven minutes out of the georgian capital. "Well holy fuck," she quickly punched in Eldridge contracting and seconds later Google gave confirmation, that company was also located in Druid Park Georgia.

She was so engrossed in her thoughts and wondering what to do with the information that the loud knock on the door made her jump. Her first thought was Ben and or Lisa. She opened it with a huge smile and was ready to yell hello when she stopped short, it was the investigating detective from earlier that morning when

the head had landed on her windshield.

"Oh hi," she said, her disappoi-
intment evident.

"Expecting someone else?" He
asked.

"Yes I was," she replied in
disdain, "is that allowed?"

"Certainly," he replied, "could
I come in?"

Donna stepped back and held
the door open wider.

He walked into the room and
told her he was sorry to be a bother but had a picture and hoped
she might be able to identify the
person in it.

Shrugging she told him she was
willing to try.

He removed a picture from an
envelope and handed it over. It
was a picture of a man laying do-

wn, he had a white sheet pulled up to his neck.

Donna recognized him immediately, she had see a picture of him earlier that morning while running on a check on LateShift's tour bus driver. "That's Len Stillwell," Donna told the detective. "He's the tour bus driver for my husband's band."

Was! Detective Ramurez replied matter of factly, "that is the head that landed on your windshield this morning."

35

*T*he detective was long gone but Donna was still reeling. The head landing on her windshield had been no accident and she felt sick. Whoever was doing this was on a reign of terror and still the police didn't believe it, the detective had been clear that they would n't write a missing persons report for the band for another few hours yet.

It was a half hour before Donna could think straight again, she walked over to the desk and stared at the computer screen.

She realized the mistake she had made, assuming that truck Ben found in Texas would be registered and insured there, she had only checked that state, it made even more sense that whoever was behind all of this was from the place that 'LateShift' was heading, where they would be performing their last concert.

She brought up MapQuest again and found directions for Eld - ridge Contracting. Just as the last

i was dotted Donna heard a knock on the door. She couldn't have
been happier to see Ben standing there, she immediately burst
into tears.

Ben pulled her into his arms,
"dude hey, it's okay"

"I'm so happy to see you," she
sobbed.

"Me too, are you ok?" He asked.

Donna nodded, "I'm over tired, everything that's happened,
the detective was here, the head
that landed on my windshild was
'LateShift's' bus driver."

"Seriously?" Ben asked in horror.

Donna nodded, "I identifed
him."

Ben shook his head, "the guys
are in big trouble."

"I don't even want to think about it but I have a feeling this is far worse than we thought."

"I do too," Ben replied.

There was another knock on the door and as Donna went to answer it she told Ben it was likly Lisa.

Ben looked at his watch and told Donna she wouldn't be landing for another ten minutes. "I spoke to her while we were both in the air." Ben said.

Opening the door Donna found a woman fron concierge Services standing there.

"Are you Mrs. Gardner?" The young lady asked.

"Yes."

Holding out a long white envelope she told Donna the letter was to be delivered to her.

"Thank you," Donna told her closing the door. Walking toward Ben she ripped open the envelope.

When her face went as white as a sheet and she began to shake Ben asked what was in the letter.

"Money," she told Ben, "they want money, the guys were kidnapped for ransom."

36

*I*t was very short and to the point. A demand for four millions dollars, one for each of the band members and for their safe return. It was suggested that the money be acquired while waiting for further instructions as to the how and where the trade would happen.

Ben and Donna were pouring over the note when there was another knock on the door. "I hope that's Lisa," she told Ben heading to the door.

It was. They shared a tearful hug at the door as did Lisa and Ben, then they sat down to compare notes. First Donna told Lisa of the ordel with the head on her windshield.

Lisa could not believe it, "I know I would have had a heart attack, she told them. "Right on the freakin' spot."

Ben told them about his trip to the county jail, Lisa and Donna were both shocked that Lou had been arrested for drug charges.

"He didn't seem like that kind of person," Donna told them.

Ben shrugged, "I met him for the first time this morning and I wouldn't have thought anything but he admitted it." He went on to tell them about finding the truck parked behind the Houston Atrodome. Both women had to stifle giggles as he told the story of breaking into the truck.

"That must have hurt," Lisa told him, "are you sure you're ok?"

"I'm fine," he said ruefully, "that will reach me not to act like superman."

"But you are a super man," Donna told him.

"Dude thanks, " that's the kindest thing I've heard in a while."

Lisa laughed, "I'll bet Amy feels the same way." She went

on to tell her two companions of her trip to Canada and how she was able to locate Karen Olewsky's roommate.

"Good job," Donna praised.

"Thank you," she beamed.

"That was good work," Ben chimed in, "what did you find out out?"

Lisa went on to tell them all about Karen Olewsky and her boyfriend, she explained about going back to the roadstop and seeing the place where the murder occurred, then about the police station where the truck smashed the Solstice and then the journey to Canada, she described the awful home that Karen Olewsky lived in and how she arrived there and heard the kid screaming for a while before the woman showed up.

Donna shook her head in disgust, "I don't know how anybody could do that to a child."

"Ben was ouraged, "that poor kid was screaming for a few minutes before you got there?" He asked.

Lisa nodded. "I know, I couldn't believe it. If I ever found out one of my kids had done that with my grandchild they would be visiting their child at my house for the rest of their lives."

Donna laughed, she knew how much Lisa and her husband loved their grandchildren, but she also knew that was unlikely to happen, Lisa's kids were responsible, loving parents.

"So the mother finally shows up?" Ben asked.

Nodding Lisa told him yes, "she said she had to get smokes, but the door was locked and the kid was fine. We went in, the place stunk, oh my god, I thought I was going to puke, and trust me I've barfed enough in the last few hours."

"You've beeen sick?" Donna asked in concern.

Lisa blushed, "it was something I ate," she told them, "nothing serious." There was no way she would ever admit to eating those paczkies, Donna wouldn't ever let her live it down and Lisa knew it. She continued hurriedly, "so I tell this woman Karen Olewsky is dead and she started to laugh, I was shocked, I could not freakin' believe it, I'm like lady are you for real?"

Donna suggested maybe she was in shock.

Lisa shrugged, "I don't know, it seemed like she didn't care. I don't think she liked Karen too much, she didn't say a good thing about her or her boyfriend."

"Did you learn anything about him?" Ben asked.

"I did," Lisa told him with a grin, "I even have a picture of the two of them." As she searched through her purse she went on, "I was told he didn't have any money, it sounded like he might have abused her too."

"Huh!" Donna exclaimed, but she didn't seem impressed with any thing she had heard so far, Lisa had not told them anything that would lead them to the men.

Lisa pulled the photo out of

her purse, but before she handed it to Donna she told them she had forgotten the most important part.

"What's that?" Ben asked.

"They left for the states a few weeks ago." She paused for a moment then added, "in his truck, an old green pickup."

"What?" Donna screamed.

"Ben gave a low whisle.

Lisa handed the picture to Donna, she looked at the picture, looked over to Lisa, then Ben and said, "I don't fuckin' believe it."

37

"What?" Ben asked. "Do you recognize them?"

Donna nodded and handed him the photo, "you will too."

Ben looked at it, frowned, held it a little closer, the looked back at Donna. "Is that Rick Eldridge?"

"Yes it is."

"I thought he was still in pris-on."

Donna shrugged, "I haven't gi-ven him any thought in years, it makes sen......" she didn't finish the sentence, she jumped up and ran to the desk that her comput-er sat on, "I knew this name sounded familar," she yelled. "I knew it, it was nagging at me but I couldn't figure it out."

Snatching her pad off the desk she turned to Ben and Lisa, "I did a search on those two names you found in the truck, it took me fo-rever because I wrongly assum-med I was looking for names loc-ated in Texas, I ended up having to do a country wide search and finally found these two names in Georgia, the addresses for both are at a place called Druid Park it's only about eleven minutes south of here."

"Dude we have to go out there and snoop around."

Donna nodded, "I think so too."

"Wait a minute," Lisa protested, "who's name is that?"

"I'm sorry,"Donna apologized, "I forgot you wouldn't know about Rick." She went on to tell the story of how about four years ago at a Canada Day Celebration Rick and his brother had tried to kill 'LateShift' by planting a bomb under the stage they were to be playing on.

Ben continued the story, "it was Donna and Isaura's quick thinking that saved the band and as it turned out it had been Rick and his brother behind the entire plan."

"That's the same Rick in that picture?" Lisa asked.

"Yes it is," Donna replied. "I guess he's out of prison and looking for revenge."

"Why would he and his brother want to kill the band?"

"At one time he had been their drummer but they fired him."

"That's how I met Donna and the band," Ben told Lisa. "I was an unpaid summer intern working for a small newspaper, they sent me to do an interview with the band, I did it and shortly after all hell broke loose, they had begun to evacuate the park but I climbed a tree and began taking pictures. It was that article and the pictures that started my career."

"Really!" Lisa exclaimed.

"Ben won awards for that art-
cle," Donna told her proudly, "he
"was a very hot commodity after
that."

Putting his arm around Donna
fondly he told Lisa about the
award her and Isaura had received. "They were given commond-
tions for bravery by the Chief of
Police."

"Good for you," Lisa told her,
"I'm so proud of you."

Blushing Donna told her thanks. "Let's go check out this address."

It was twenty minutes before
they could get out of the hotel
parking lot, there had been a fen-
der bender and until the two vehicles were moved they had to

wait.

Donna was impatient and kept slapping the steering wheel, "lets go," she would yell.

While they were waiting Ben typed the address into the GPS system. "We're good to go when it's clear," he told Donna.

Seconds later a tow truck pulled out of the lot with one of the cars behind it and they were able to drive out of the lot.

The voice on the GPS system instructed her to turn right. With in a moment it was telling her to take another right and follow Morningside Drive for 1.6 miles.

"It seems funny hearing something in miles doesn't it?" Donna asked.

"It's always in miles," Lisa told her.

"Not in Canada," Donna laughed, "we use the metric system."

"That's right I forgot about that." Lisa replied.

"Every time we talk about the weather I try to convert from celcius to degrees, just for you Lisa."

"Thank you, you are so sweet."

"No, I just know how easily you get confused," Donna told her laughing.

When you look this good, knowing the difference between degrees and ......what was that other word?" Lisa asked.

Donna looked in the rear view mirror, "seriously?" she asked.

Lisa grinned, "no, of course I know the word."

Turn right at the next road," Ben instructed Donna interrupting the goood natured banter.

"Thanks Ben," Lisa giggled, "I think you just saved me."

"It was Celsius," Donna called back, not taking her eyes off the road.

"This should be Dan Johnson Road coming up on the left," Ben told her. The GPS confirmed that it was seconds later.

"We want number 1030, keep your eyes open," Donna told her companions.

Ben looked around, "it sure is secluded out here."

Donna nodded, "we are definately out in the country, there aren't that many houses."

"There's a mail box," Lisa shouted, "there's a number on it."

Donna slowed down and they all peered out the window, "245"

Ben called out, "we're a long way away yet."

Donna sped up and they passed a few properties before she slowed again.

"761," Lisa told them.

They drove another two miles before seeing another home, the further they went the fewer houses there were.

"It feels like we're in the middle of nowhere," Donna told her friends, I hope we aren't wasting our time, my husband is missing and we might be on a wild goose chase."

Ben reached over and rubbed her arm in reassurance, "we will find him, we'll find all of them hang in there."

'There's a mailbox," Lisa called up front.

"Where?" Donna asked looking around, "I don't see one."

"Pull over to the left," Lisa told her, "it's almost covered by trees, I'll look at the number."

Donna had no sooner come to a stop when Lisa opened the door and jumped out, her and Ben watched as Lisa pulled aside some dense low bushes to reveal a mailbox."

"Dude, she's like totally amazing, Ben marveled. "I didn't see it."

"Me neither," Donna told him.

Lisa jumped back in the SUV, "1028," she told them.

"How in the hell did you see that?" Donna asked, "you are good."

Lisa laughed, "years of spottting a good shoe sale from the

other side of the store, it's a tal-
ent, I have a number of them,
that is only one on a long list."

"That long list is missing good
cook," Donna kidded good natu-
redly.

"Trophy wives don't cook," Lisa
replied in mock horror.

Ben and Donna laughed.

"Shit!" Donna exclaimed, "we've
come to the end of the road. Her
frustration was visible and her
eyes welled with tears. "I wonder if those were dummy addresses."

"Let's get out and take a look
around," Ben suggested.

The three of them jumped out
of the Suv, it appeared as though
there wasn't a house in sight and
they had reached a dead end
with a steel barrier blocking the

road.

They looked around, no numbers or mailboxes, no houses, the area seemed deserted.

"Maybe we missed it," Lisa suggested, "why don't we drive back and look?"

Ben agreed, "I think that's a good idea."

Ten minutes later they all agreed that they had missed nothing, 1030 should have been near where the road ended. They had turned around and gone back to the end of the road and the three of them were standing out on the road again.

"Look at that," Ben told them pointing to the left, the barrier has an opening and the trees do look a little more sparse, they have more of an overhang than anything but I think you could drive throught there."

"Ya think?" Donna asked, look-kng at him like he was out of his mind.

"Dude seriously, I think you could drive through there. Give me the keys, I'll do it."

A minute later they had driven through the barrier and were going through a cutaway in the trees.

"Holy shit!" Donna exclaimed, "from where we were standing it didn't look like we'd be able to fit through there but there was a ton of room."

"This is regularly traveled too," Ben told them, "you can tell by the tire tracks, we're not the only vehicle in here recently."

"Five minutes later they came to a large clearing, in front of then was an enormous steel building, it had no windows, it was very long, with a rounded roof and the front of it had industrial size doors, both secured with a large padlock.

To the left of that was a small shed and a collection of miscellaneos junk in front, a rusty lawnmower, a few old gas cans, an old plow that was overgrown with weeds and two bikes laying carelessy off to the side.

On the right off the property were two vehicles, an old car, that looked like it hadn't moved in years, weeds and grasss had grown up to the windows, the windshield was covered in dirt and appeared as though many a bird had perched on it over the years, their droppings were everywhere. Beside it was a later model truck, black, it looked as though it hadn't been sitting there that long. Next to both the vehicles was an industrial sized tank sitting on a platform and stilts about ten feet in the air. In front of that was a pile of gravel that looked freshly dumped.

"Look over there," Lisa yelled from the back seat.

"What?" Both Donna and Ben asked at the same time.

Lisa was pointing far to the right and now almost behind them, there clear as day was a hand painted sign that said Eldridge Contracting.

Donna's heart was pounding so hard she couldn't breathe.

"This place has some connection to the band's disappearance."

Ben agreed, "yes, it has to, this address was registered to the truck that I know that replacement driver drove. "

"And," Donna added, "it's bears the same last name as somebody we know has a vendetta against Paul and the guys and we know he was heading to the states and we know he was driving a truck just like the one that has been terrorizing us for two days."

"Why don't we get out and take a look around," Lisa suggested as she opened her door and jumped down to the ground.

"I hope nobody shows up," Donna said worriedly, she glanced around nervously expecting at any moment another vehicle to drive into the clearing, a green truck perhaps.

"To be on the safe side I don't think we should leave this truck out in the open, we better hide it somehow." Ben told Donna.

"Where?"

Ben pointed to some trees ahead of them, "if I drive over there we can throw some branches over it, not an ideal plan but better than nothing."

Donna was agreement, "let's do that."

Rolling down his window he told Lisa what they were going to do. By the time he had driven the SUV as far into the bushes as it would go, Lisa was there pulling branches off trees and piling them behind the truck to hide it from view.

"That's about the best we're going to do," Ben told the ladies, "let's go for a walk and see what we can find."

The three friends headed off toward the small shack on their left, they had to navigate through the junk scattered in front and the weeds were up to their knees.

"What does poison Ivy look like?" Lisa asked.

"I'm not sure," Ben told her.

"Donna shook her head, "me neither, I should know but I can only identify the end result not the cause."

Ben was rattling the door of the shack, "it should open he told the women, 'it's not locked or any thing, at least not out here."

Donna walked to the side of the small building and tried looking in a window. It was so dirty she couldn't see a thing. "Damn," she cursed.

"He's in," Lisa called out, "Donna come here."

Racing back to the front she was right behind Lisa as she followed Ben inside.

The bulding was all but empty, there was a long shelf with various cans of paint, cleaners, a solvent an old yellow hard hat, it smelled dank and musty but otherwise there was nothing else in it.

"Shit," Donna swore. "This is so frustrating."

"They walked out and back into the bright sunlight, all three of them shading their eyes against the bright light.

"I guess we check out that," Ben told them pointing toward the long steel building."

Donna and Lisa followed him toward it, they walked up to the double steel doors and began tugging on the pad lock, it was of an industrial size and getting past it was not going to happen. That didn't stop Ben from yanking on the lock and throwing his weight against the door.

"There's no way," Donna told him, "it's designed to keep people like us out."

"Crappers!" Ben shouted. "We have to be able to get in here some how."

"Let's go around back, we may find something back there." Donna suggested.

The weeds were up to their knees and they had to step over lengths of pipe, Donna didn't see a piece of barbed wire and when she stepped on one side of it the entire piece flipped up and scratched her arm.

"I hope you've had your tetnus shot," Lisa told her.

"I do."

"Ouch crap!" Lisa complained, "some of the weeds have god dam thorns and they're killing my freakin' legs."

"I can't imagine walking in those heels is very comfortable either," Donna laughed.

"Heels are one of my specialiaties," Lisa replied.

"Of course as a trophy wife that would be important, it must be part of the job."

"It is," Lisa replied with a nod, "and you know I'm a desperate housewife of Milan Michigan."

"Of course you are, I would expect no less."

They were so involved in their good natured banter they didn't realize Ben was no longer with them.

"Where the hell could he have gone?" Donna asked, looking around.

Lisa shrugged, "he was just here."

Donna's heart began to pound, "Ben?" She called out. No answer. She was becoming frantic, "oh god Lisa, what if something happened to him. "BEN," she screamed.

"Dude, hey I'm up here."

Shielding their eyes Donna and

Lisa looked up to see Ben standing on the roof of the steel buildding.

"How in the hell did you get up there?" Donna demanded.

Ben pointed down and to side of the building, "That ladder," he told them grinning. Sure enough, built into the side, it stretched from a foot off the ground to the roof.

"I didn't even see that, did you?" Donna asked, turning to Lisa.

She shook her head, "I missed it."

As Ben scambled down the ladder, part of it separated from the wall and swung out a few inches, it was so unexpected, one of Ben's legs slipped off a rung and he looked like he was about

to fall, "crappers," he shouted.
Regaining his balance he quickly
scrambled to the ground, grinning he told then that was totally
awesome.

"Donna playfully punched him
in the arm, "you scared the hell
out of us."

"Sorry dude," he said ruefully,
"that wasn't my intention."

"Was there anything up there?" Donna asked.

"Believe it or not yes, pieces
of pipe, some bricks, rusty tools
and an old fire extinguisher, no
way to get in though."

"Let's go to the far side and
see what's there."

This thing is locked up pretty
good, there must be something
important in there." Ben remarked.

"Hey," Donna shouted, "I bet it's a grow op."

Ben shook his head, "no it can't be, that would take a lot of electricity, there isn't enough going into this building." He point - ed to the one wire and box near the roof line, "if this was a grow op there would be boxes and wires everywhere and I think we'd here fa......."

" Ssh," Lisa cautioned, "I can hear something."

They all stopped and sure enough they could hear a vehicle approaching, within seconds it would be in the clearing and the three of them would easily be seen.

"Come on," Ben yelled, "let's go."

The three of them raced to

the other end of the building and Donna layed flat down on the round and peeked around the corner. A couple seconds later a vehicle drove into the clearing and the occupants jumped out.

"I don't fuckin' believe it," she whispered. "Holy fuck!."

38

*B*en helped Donna to her
feet and asked what was wrong,
she was shaking and as white as
a sheet.

"Dude what is it?"

"Take a look," she told him.
He got down on the ground

and carefully peered around the corner, what he saw took the breath out of him. An old green GMC Suburuban truck was parked in the clearing and walking toward the building was the former drummer for 'LateShift,' Rick Eldridge and his psychotic brother Bobby. Suddenly everything fell into place.

Ben stood up and hugged Donna, "we know who's behind all this now, we're going to find the guys."

Donna carefully looked around the edge of the building, the two men were talking animately although Donna couldn't make out what they were saying, then to her surprise they turned back to the truck, got in and left.

"We can look around some

more before we go to the police," Ben told her. "Look there
are doors on this end too."

"And the same kind of padlock,
we'll never get in." Donna replied glumly.

"You guys come here," Lisa
called out.

She was fifteen feet away,
squatting down looking at the
ground. "What?" Donna asked.
Her and Ben walked over and
knelt beside her.

She pointed to the trees, "this
side is almost the same as the
one we drove through, look, a vehicle could drive in this way too,
what she was showing them was
now an obvious clearing. "Check
out these tracks too, aren't they
huge? I mean bigger than your
average trucks?"

"Crappers! Are they ever, Ben exclaimed, a bus could have driven through he......"
They all looked at each other

then jumped to their feet.
"Look how long this buiding is you guys, the bus is in there oh my god it's in there," Donna screamed.

38

*B*en, Lisa and Donna

raced to the dooors and banged on the them, they yanked at the padlock but it was clear they we-re not going to get in."

"There must be a way," Donna

yelled frantically, "we're getting into this building."

"I think we'll have to get the police out here," Ben told her, "they can handle it from here."

"No way," Donna told him adamantly, "they won't get involved yet, if we leave here we're wasting time."

Resigned, Ben gave in. "Ok, what are we going to do?"

"We're getting in there and I don't care how we do it."

Ben laughed, "Ok let's go in."

Surprised Donna asked him what he meant.

"I mean we're going in."

"How?"

"We'll drive."

Donna was perplexed, "how do you plan to do...." Ben was gone before she could finish the sentence he was jogging toward the hidden SUV.

"What is he doing?" Lisa ask-ed.

Donna began to laugh, "I think he plans to drive that thing right through these doors."

"You've got to be freakin' kid-ding." Lisa gasped.

Donna shook her head, "no, I don't think so."

She watched as Ben pulled the branches off the truck then backed out and headed toward them. As he approached he wav - ed them out of the way.

Ben turned the vehicle around so he was facing the building, he backed up then stepped on the gas. The Suv shot forward and smashed into the steel doors wi-th a sickening crunch. They didn't give way though, in fact other than a few scratches they seemed to sustain little damage.

He backed up again and took another run at it, this time fastter. He rammed the doors with a bang and they did give a little, still, he wasn't able to break through.

"Shit," Donna swore, "the SUV is liable to give out before those doors do."

Lisa nodded, "I was thinking the same thing."

Ben backed up again, just before he put his foot on the gas Donna and Lisa both heard a vehicle, it was coming in behind Ben and was going to drive into the clearing within a minute or two.

"Oh shit," Donna yelled, she

began running toward the Ben and waving her arms.

"He rolled down the window and asked what was wrong.

"There's someone coming," she panted breathlessly, "now what?"

Ben thought for a second then yanked the keys out of the ignition, jumped out of the Suv and yelled come on.

Lisa and Donna followed him back around the side of the building that that they had just come from, "climb the ladder quick," he told Lisa, Donna and I'll hold it for you."

The second she was on the roof he told Donna to go, "no way she said, you're going to be stuck down here."

"No I won't I'll be right be

behind you."

She shook her head, "I'm not leaving you."

Ben looked toward the trees, the sound was so close he knew the vehicle would drive into the clearing within a couple seconds. "Donna we don't have time you have to go," he pleaded.

So unnaccustomed to hearing him sound like that Donna got on the ladder and made her way to the top, she was only a couple of rungs away from the roof when the top gave way and she could feel herself falling backwards.

"Give me your hand," Lisa hissed, "quick."

Donna reached out and in the nick of time Lisa was able to pull her in, another second and it would have been too late, she would have landed on her back twelve feet below.

It was too late for Ben though, and Donna and Lisa watched in horror as Ben pulled as hard as he could and ripped the ladder off the wall, he jumped out of the way as it hit the ground, then he ran, he knew he was in trouble but he took comfort knowing that Rick and Bobby would be unable to reach Lisa and Donna. It was going to buy him time until he could think up a plan.

39

*T*ime seemed to stand still for a moment, Donna couldn't believe her and Lisa were on a building with no way down and Ben was probably running for his life.

Think, she told herself, *you have to do something fast.*

Her and Lisa ran toward the end of the bulding then dropped to their knees and watched the clearing, a second later the green GMC Suburban appeared and came to a stop directly behind the SUV.

Donna sucked in her breath, she was paralyzed with with fear, she couldn't believe after all these years she was about to do battle with these thugs again.

"I'm going to kill that fuckin' bitch," this time, Bobby was telling his half brother, "I should have done it years ago."

"You said this was going to be easy," Rick complained, "when I called you with the idea you told me this was a better way, you promised."

"Quit the fuckin' whining you know I fuckin' hate that."

"They can't be far," Rick told him as he opened the door of the SUV. He looked in the front and back seats then went to the back and opened the hatch. "I thought they might be hiding in there."

"That would be pretty stupid of them now wouldn't it?" Bobby scoffed. "Fuck your stupid."

They continued arguing as they made their way around the far side of the bulding and Donna heaved a sigh of relief, "if they had seen that ladder they would probably have figured out we're up here."

"But how are we going to get down now?" Lisa asked.

Donna shrugged, "the fuck if I

know."

As the truck had driven into the clearing Ben made his way to the far side of the building, he watched the two men go through the SUV and heard them arguing, their voices faded as they walked in the opposite direction and Ben began to make his way back. He stepped over the ladder, quickly realizing Lisa and Donna had no way to get off of the roof, *crap – pers*, he thought, *how do I get them down.* He chastised himself for acting before thinking, *you are an idiot Benjamin Ross,* he said to himelf. *Now think.*

When he got back to the end of the bulding, he carefully peer-ed around the side to make sure the two men weren't there, he was relieved to see they were no where in sight. Quickly making a calculation he thought he had a way to get the women down, it was dicey, but it was all he had.

He looked up to see both Donna and Lisa looking over the edge. Holding up his index finger to indicate he wanted a minute he went back to the corner of the building, he wanted to know exactly where Rick and Bobby were before he tried anything, he could see them, a couple hundred feet away, searching for the three people they knew were hiding close by.

Good, Ben thought, *I have a bit time.* He turned back and looked up to see Lisa waving him over.

"Be careful, stay right where you are, we're throwing a couple of things down." She whispered loudly.

Ben watched as a brick landed on the ground, then a foot long piece of pipe, the fire extinguisher he had seen earlier fell with a loud thud and finally a hammer. *"Smart ladies* he thought with a smile, *giving us weapons.*

He quickly gathered them and threw them into the back seat of the SUV, then ran to the side of the building again, Rick and Bobby were walking toward the large sign that said "Eldridge Contracting, *they probably think we're behind that,* he thought, *good, I have enough time.*

He knew he had to tell Lisa and Donna what he was planning because the moment he started the SUV those guys would be running their way. Ben walked over to the building and looking up at the two faces staring down at him whispered his plan.

"Shut up! Lisa exclaimed. "Are you for real?"

"Dude, it's the only way."

"He's right, Donna told her, "we have to do it."

Ben nodded, "and we're going to do it now, we can't wait." He ran to the rented vehicle, put the keys in the ignition and the moment it started he stepped on the gas pedal and brought it to a stop just short of the doors. He held his breath and waited for what seemed like an eternity, then watched as Lisa landed on the hood, it was a relatively soft fall, she was in excellent physical shape and years of working out had paid off. He was worried about Donna, she was not in great physical shape, she wasn't agile like Lisa and he hoped she wouldn't break something in the fall. *Come on* he prayed j*ump,* he watched as Lisa coaxed her and hoped she would do it before Rick and Bobby came around the corner, he figured that would be any second. *Crappers Donna jump, do it,* he pleaded silently.

Seconds later she fell on the hood. It was a harder landing than Lisa's and not nearly as elegant, he could tell by the pained look on her face that it hurt too.

As Lisa was helping her off the hood Rick and Bobby came around the corner, "GET IN," Ben screamed.

Lisa yanked the back door open and her and Donna scrambled in, the moment they pulled the door shut Ben hit the lock button.

A second later both Rick and Bobby were banging on the winows and kicking the SUV, "you son of a bitch," Bobby was screaming. His eyes were bugging out of his head and his face was scarlet red, his rage was palpable.

"They've got us now," Lisa muttered, "we're screwed. Why don't you drive away Ben, why are you just sitting here?"

Ben turned to look at her, "they have no weapons, they can't get in here, at least not in the next couple of minutes and we're not going to leave before finding out if the bus is in that building, and if it is I suspect Paul, Ron, Scott and Andy and in there with it."

"So what are we going to do? Donna asked. "Cause they will get in here in eventually."

Ben agreed, "I have an idea though, we'll have to work toge-ether to pull it off though, are you in?"

"I am, Donna told him, "I'm not leaving without getting in that building."

Reluctantly Lisa agreed, "so what's the plan?"

As they listened then strateg-ized, Rick and Bobby continued to bang on the windows, at one point Rick tried the same thing Ben had in Houston and with the same results, he ended up rolling on the ground in pain.

"This is the perfect time," Ben

told them, "one of them is already down on the ground, are you
ready?"

Both women nodded and Donna handed Ben the hammer they
had thrown off the roof, Lisa
took the pipe and Donna chose
the fire extinguisher.

"One, two, three, ready go,"
Ben called out and hit the button
to unlock the doors.

The moment Lisa heard the
click she kicked her door open,
Bobby was standing close enough that the force knocked him
off balance giving Lisa enough
time to get out of the truck and
tackle him.

Donna went out the other side
with the fire extinguisher in her
hand, Rick was still rolling on the
ground in pain.

Ben stayed in the SUV as they had all agreed and the moment it was safe to do so he was going to drive through those doors.

Lisa was strugging with Bobby, her intent was to move him away from the vehicle but he wasn't an easy match, he was laying on the ground on his back and grabbed her hair at the scalp, he yanked her head down to his face, "I "am going to kill you, you fucking cunt," he hissed.

"I don't friggin' think so," Lisa told him with a smirk, "you're not man enough for that job."

That statement infuriated Bobby, without thinking he let go of her hair and with his other hand slammed his fist into her right cheek. She was dazed but for no more than a second.

"You prick," she screamed and wrapping both hands around the pipe she was holding Lisa slammed it into Bobby's face. She was strong, the pipe connected with bone, there was a sickening crack and Bobby lay still.

Ben put the SUV in drive and drove into the doors, they moved inward slightly and groaned but still wouldn't give, he backed up and tried again, the sound of metal striking metal was ear shattering and this time he saw the padlock bust. "Finally," he yelled. He put the truck in reverse and backed up a little further, "this time I'm going through," he said determinedly.

Donna was standing over top of Rick, he was still in too much pain to move. "C'MON YOU ASS-

HOLE, GET THE FUCK UP." She screamed. "I DARE YOU." She kicked him and he began to cry, "you are a coward just like your brother," she yelled, "take this!" She lifted the fire extinguisher over her head and using every bit of strengh she possessed she brought it down on his head. A moment later blood began runnning out of his nose.

Ben stepped on the gas hard and the SUV went flying toward the doors, he closed his eyes and braced himself, knowing he was putting his life in jeopardy, the truck hit the doors at forty miles an hour and finally gave way, it happened so fast Ben didn't realize he was in until he noticed the darkness. Then he saw the bus.

40

*T*hey found Ron in a far corner, his back was against the steel wall, he was dazed, confused and barely coherent, he kept muttering "I can hear Mrs. G, I can hear Mrs. G." His jeans were worn through at the knees and blood was caked around the material, the palms of his hands were raw, his face was badly bruised and Donna thought he had a broken nose.

It was clear Scott was long dead, his skull was crushed and he was barely recognizable, just to be sure Donna felt for a pulse, but there was nothing, he was stiff, cold and very white and Donna told them he'd been gone for many many hours.

Andy was alive, but just barely, his pulse was weak and thready and it was clear he needed immediate medical intervention. "I'm unable to do anything for him, he needs to be in a hospital," Donna said.

"I've called the police, hopefully there will be an ambulance here shortly." Ben replied.

They found Paul in what appeared to be a shallow shaft of
some kind, he was laying in a cr-
umpled heap about four feet in
the ground.

Donna didn't hesitate and with
a cry jumped in beside him. She
knew he was alive, she was able
to hear his shallow breathing, he
had a nasty gash on his head and
it looked like he had lost a lot of
blood, it was still bleeding prof-
usely and that concerned her, ju-
dging how dry some of the blood
was, it appeared that he had fall-
en hours ago, that he was still losing blood told her it was a very
deep cut and that much blood
loss could be life threatening.

"Could one of you look on the
bus for a first aid kit?" She asked,
"I need to stop some bleeding."

It was obvious he had at least one broken leg and his stomach had been pierced by what she assumed was a jagged piece of concrete, that concerned her, it looked dangerously close to his kidneys and she was concerned about Sepsis.

Neither Ben or Lisa could find a kit, but they had found a sheet and a pair of scissors and cut long strips of cloth for her to use as bandages. "Thanks," she told them, "please get some water for Ron, I think he's suffering from dehydration and it's stifling hot in here."

What about Andy?" Lisa asked.

"I'm sure he needs water to but he's unconscious and won't be able to swallow, he'll aspirate anything that goes into his mouth and choke to death."

"Oh, ok." Lisa replied.

"Don't worry, as soon as the paramedics get here they'll put him on a drip and hydrate him."

"Dude, Ben replied, "I'm a layman what did you just say?"

Donna laughed, "they'll give him fluids intraveneously."

She had no sooner finished wrapping Paul's head in a make-shift tournequet when the sound of sirens broke the air.

Epilogue

1

*I*t had been an exhausting two weeks since arriving back in Canada. They had attended three funerals, the first for Scott, then Isaura's and finally Andy's today, he had sucuumbed to his inj – ries nine days after being airlift- ed from Atlanta to a hospital in Oshawa.

Now they were gathered at the Pristin home northeast of

Toronto.

Paul was wearing two casts, one on his left arm the other on his right leg, he had broken both when he fell into the shaft. He had lost an enormous amount of blood and had to be given transfusions when he arrived at the hospital, they discovered a hairline fracture too but he was expected to make a full recovery. They never were able to find out why that narrow hole was there.

As Donna had suspected, Ron did have a broken nose, as they later discovered it was from walking into a metal hoist. He also suffered a mild concussion and had been suffering from dedydration but he too would make a full recovery.

Bobby died from the injury he sustained, not from being smashed in the face but after he stupidly threw himelf in front of the truck just before it was driven through the doors of the steel of the building.

Ben was convinced that Bobby had stupidly believed he would stop if he jumped in front of the truck. The truth was Ben hadn't realized he'd flung himself in front of the SUV, the last time he saw Bobby alive he was laying on the ground with Lisa standing over him.

Rick had suffered serious injuries that required facial reconsttion, the bones on one side of his face had been completely shattered when he was struck with the fire extinguisher. The surgeon had done his best but Rick had been told he would never look the same. Not that it would matter to him, he most likely would never get out of prison.

The Medical Examiner would tell them that Scott had died from trauma to his body that included his skull being crushed, they were assured that he would not have suffered and most likely died instantly.

2

*D*onna put her hand on her head and sank back in the chair, "I'm glad this day is almost over."

"So am I," Paul told her with tears in his eyes, I can't believe Andy's gone too now"

Donna nodded, "when they

said they were sending him back here I thought he was was going to make it."

Paul looked at Ron sadly," it's just the two of us."

Ron sat quietly, he didn't respond other than nodding at Paul.

Ben told them again how sorry he was. "I wish I could have done more."

Paul put his hand up, "Ben please, you've did so much, you could have come straight home but even after being away from your family for months you went to Atlanta to see us and it if not for your help we'd all be dead."

Donna agreed, "you were amazing Ben, you were too Lisa."

"All in a day's work," she laughed, a long freakin' day."

"Is Kirk pissed about the Solstice?" Donna asked.

"He was until his knew one ar

rived."

"What?" How"

Lisa pointed at Jim Pristin, "he bought Kirk a new one."

"That was so nice of you Jim," Donna told him, "you are so generous."

"I'm nothing of the sort," he replied, "he deserved it, if it weren't for Lisa using it to get to Attlanta it would still be in Kirk's driveway."

"The best part," Lisa laughed, "is I didn't have to clean the back of that car."

"Clean it?" Donna asked.

Lisa face turned red, "it got a little dirty on the way to Georgia, water bottles, a few protein bar wraps." She shuddered thinking of the pazckies, Lisa never wanted to think of those disgusting deep fried hunks of dough again.

"Are you ok?" Donna asked.

"Yes why?"

"Your shivering.

No, no I'm fine," Lisa assured her, "I was just thinking of all that happened."

"It's remarkable really," Jim told them, "how the three of you came together as a team, put all the pieces together and found the guys."

"We do work well together," Ben told them, "if the circumstances hadn't been so tragic it may have been fun."

"Donna agreed, "it was tragic, I still can't believe we've lost Is - aura, Scott and now Andy."

"So their motivation was money?" Jim asked.

"I'm sorry to interrupt, Madeline Pristin said as she entered the room, "I thought you would enjoy a snack."

"Thank you Maddy," Jim told

his wife fondly.

"Yes thank you," Donna replied, "those are my favorite."

Lisa took one look at the jelly donuts and ran to the bathroom.

Back to the question Jim "yes," Donna said, "Rick was holding a grudge since he got out of jail a year ago, he was working at a bar in Oshawa, some dive on Simcoe Street, he quit and then got a hold of Bobby, the two of them came up with this scheme to grab the tour bus and hold the men for ransom."

"What happened?" Jim asked with a frown. "Why did so many people have to die?"

Donna shook her head sadly "the two of them are idiots that's why."

Paul interrupted, "I don't remember to much of what happenened other than a guy in a mask was on the bus, then it gets foggy.

He opened a canister and there was an awful smell, Ron told them."

Then what?" Donna asked.

Ron shrugged, "I vaguely remember waking up and there was fighting and yelling, I think it might have been Andy and Scott."

Donna nodded and picked up the story, "Rick seemed eager to talk, that was him wearing the mask, it was a gas that knocked you all out, we still don't know what kind, I doubt we ever will."

"What about the bus driver?" Jim asked.

"The phony or the one whose head landed on my windshield."

Jim shuddered at the thought.

Donna answered him, "according to Rick they grabbed Len Stilwell while the band was still on stage, he indicated there was a very incompetent security guard that made things really easy for them"

Ben picked up the story, "he admitted his incompetence, he's no longer employed."

"Good," was the quick reply from Paul, "if he'd done his job properly everyone might still be alive."

Ben agreed, "that's why he doesn't have a job, he won't be working as a security guard any time soon."

"So," Jim continued, "they were able to grab the bus driver and put their own in."

"Yes," Donna replied, she got up and walked over to the window, she didn't want anyone to see the tears. "Jim Reigns is his name, he was an employee of Eldride Contacting."

Paul got up and hobbled over to Donna, "are you ok?" He asked.

"Yes," she told him wiping her eyes, "'I'll be ok."

"If you don't want to talk about anymore you don't have to, her husband told her.

Donna was touched by his conncern, "I'm ok really," she reassured him. "I want to tell the entire story."

"Don't feel it's necessary," Jim told her, "if you're not up to it we can let it be."

"No, no I'm fine Donna insisted, "I'd like to get it out, I'm the only one who can tell the story, I'm the one that talked to Rick last week."

"Why did you do that?" Lisa asked her.

"I wanted to know everything,

I didn't want to have to wonder all my life, I had to talk to him."

"I'm glad you did," Ben told her, "I would have wondered too, I'd like to know everything."

"What do you want to know?" Donna asked him.

Why did they drop Len Stillwell's head on your windshield?"

"To scare the hell out of me, no other reason, would you believe they paid a mentally handicapped kid to do it?"

"Shut up!" Lisa yelled.

Donna nodded, "he was slow but functional enough to understand his instructions, I guess he waited for hours and just as I drove out from the underground parking lot he dropped it. He was standing on the walkway just over the exit."

Everyone in the room shook their head.

"It's a miracle he picked the right SUV, it could easily have been another vehicle," Ron told her."

"Yes but I was the unfortunate one. "

"Hey," Ron practically yelled.

All eyes turned to him. Ron looked at Paul, "do you remember at one point Andy was moaning and talking and and I told you I couldn't really understand him?"

Paul nodded. "Yeah."

Ron's voice was barely audible as he told them what he had heard Andy say, "he said he chopped it off, it rolled on the floor of the bus."

"Oh my god," Jim groaned.

"That makes sense," Donna told him, "Rick told me that Len put up a fight and Bobby used a machete to chop his head off."

Lisa gagged, "I think I'm going to be sick," she told them and ran to the bathroom again.

Ben shook his head, "it could have been as simple as a kidnaping for ransom, instead they end-up killing practically everyone."

"Even Jim Reigns," Donna replied, the cops found him in that black truck we saw parked in the clearing, they slashed his throat too."

"I thought there was a ranson request," Jim remarked looking at Donna. "Did you not receive one?"

"I did, Ben and I got it about an hour before we headed out to Eldridge Contracting, there was no use calling the police, they had already made it clear they weren't going to help us until twenty four hours was up."

"That is unacceptable," Jim roared. "Somebodies head ought to roll for that."

His statement made everyone laugh uncomfortably.

He was clearly embarrassed and quickly apologized, "I'm so sorry, I meant no disrespect."

"We know that Jim," Paul told him, "don't be sorry."

"I'm going to see what I can do down there," Jim went on, "the Atlanta Police Department has to bear some responsibililty for all this, they're incompetent."

"I wish they would have taken me seriously when Len's head fell on my windshield, even then they refused to get involved."

"Leave it with me," Jim told her. "I have some pull."

Donna nodded grimly, she almost felt sorry for the APD, if Jim were getting involved there was trouble for them in the near future.

"How much did they want," he asked.

"A million for each of them," Donna replied.

"Sons a bitches," he ranted, "I am so happy one of them is dead, it's too bad they both aren't."

Lisa came back into the room looking pale, "are you ok?" Donna asked her.

She nodded, "I'll be ok, what did I miss""

"Pretty well everything," Donna laughed, "but I think we're all done."

"I have another question," Ron said quietly, "how was Rick related to Eldridge Contracting?"

"It was his biological father's company," Donna told him, "if you remember, when Rick was a kid his parents split up, he went back and forth between his mom and dad's and when his mom re-married he gained a new dad and step brother."

"That's right," Paul said, "I remember that now."

"Was Rick's dad, his real one involved in any of this? Paul asked.

Donna shook her head, "no as a matter of fact he was away on vacation and business was carrying on as usual, in fact the police investigation show that a load of gravel was dumped there early on the morning we found you."

Ron and Paul looked at each other, "we heard that," Paul told her, "it gave us some hope but the truck was gone within a couple of minutes."

It was quiet for a couple of minutes, everyone lost in their own thoughts, Donna broke the silence. "Well if that's it I'll be happy to let this go, I'm tired of talking about it."

"I'm sorry," Lisa replied, "I do have a couple more questions."

"Go ahead," Donna told her.

"Are you sure?" Lisa asked.

"I'm sure."

Why did they they try to blow up your truck? Why was that hand waving at you and Isaura and why did they kill that Karen Olewsky?"

"Wait a minute, Donna laughed, "that's three questions."

"Lisa smiled, "but I said it all in one breath so it's really only one right?"

Trying to follow her logic Donna thought for a moment?

'This is kind of like that time you gave Scandinavia as a Province isn't it? You're just trying to throw me off here?"

"Lisa laughed, "yes that's it, of course."

Donna grinned, "they didn't want to kill us, they hoped Isaura and I would be scared and go home, Rick said they had tangled with us once before and did not want to do it again. It was Karen Olewsky waving at us, once she realized what Rick and Bobby were planning she wanted no part of it, Bobby was furious and slit her throat as soon as he realized what she was doing. Everything they did while Isaura and I were on the way to Atlanta was to scare us into going home. Bobby had Paul's cell phone and called me, at that point he just wanted to torment me."

I apologize Donna," Jim Pristin said, "but I have one more question. If they wanted a ranson why did they critically injure Scott and Andy?"

"They didn't mean to Jim, both of them put up a fight and Rick said he and Bobby were fighting back."

Ron shook his head, "I don't remember that."

"I don't either," Paul told him," "and I hope I never do."

"Donna went back over and sat down beside Paul, she lay her head on his shoulder and told them that was it. "I don't want to think about this any more."

Why don't we think of something positive and exciting," Jim suggested. "Donna, Ben, Lisa, I have a proposition for you."

3

*T*he three friends were stunned at Jim's proposition.

"You want us to open a detecctive agency?" Ben asked his father in law.

"I do son, the three of you are

naturals. How many times have the three of you been involved in and solved a mystery? Look at the outcome each time, you guys were meant to be a team."

"It sounds intriguing," Donna replied.

"What about my job?" Ben asked.

"You hate being away from your family," Jim reminded him.

"Yes I hate that part of it but I love the adventure and excitement."

"You'll have that, I can guarantee it " Jim assured him. "And you'll only cater to the rich and famous, big cases that will take you all over the world."

Ben smiled at his father in law, "Dad, if Donna and Lisa agree I'm in."

Donna was already sold on the idea, she required no more convincing. "I'm in."

Lisa wasn't so sure. "I don't know how I could do it," she told Jim, "Donna and Ben live here, they could be in the office all the time, I'm five hours away, all I could do is communicate by phone, I think I'll have to pass."

Jim shook his head, "there will be no office, when you get a client the three of you will go to him."

"That costs time and money," Lisa pointed out."

Yes it does Lisa," Jim replied, "I have the money and you have the time, aren't you just a bored housewife?"

Donna laughed, "pampered, spoiled....."

"This would take away from my shoe shopping time," Lisa quipped.

"How many pairs of shoes do

you have?" Jim asked her.

"A lot," she replied.

"Then you have enough," Jim told her. "Are you in?"

"Will I be flying around on that jet?" Lisa asked with a wink.

"All the time."

"I'm in," she replied. "Because I'll look good on a private jet in my new Jimmy Choo's."

"Wonderful," Jim told them as he clapped his hands, he handed Donna, Ben and Lisa each a box. "Here are your business cards, your new agency will be called 'Ross and Company.'

Acknowledgements

I'd like to thank each of the me-
bers of "lateShift individually for
allowing me to write about them
in four books.

Scott 'scooter' Green, a terrific
singer and all around funny
guy. I'd like to than you for giving me the opportununity to write a colorful character.

Andy 'Rockstar' Croteau, my 'go
to' guy. Your knowledge about
music especially the obsure always amazes me, thanks for sha-
ing and thanks for your friend-
ship.

Ron 'Bez' Bezener, my crotchety old friend whom I adore even if you don't like my apple pie. Thanks for many years of laughs and for all the blog topics.

Most importantly, thank you to my incredible husband for always supporting me, encouraging me and for being my soulmate. I love you.

Thanks Isaura for being a part of the 'LateShift' Mysteries. I'm sorry it ended so tragically, but I'm sure you'll understand the story must go on. Friends?

Lisa, oh Lisa what can I say? You make me laugh! I've so enjoyed the adventure we've shared and I look forward to the ones we'll have with Ben in in the 'Ross and Company Novels.'

A Preview of

Haywire

Available

December 2010

International intrigue is the order of the day when the trio from 'Ross and Company' set out to solve a very puzzling mystery.

Donna, Ben, and Lisa are sent on a wild goose chase half way around the world after one of the biggest rappers in the country Cuz 'N Troy asks the three detectives to locate his missing niece.

There is something very wrong though, when they finally bring her home he tell them she is not his niece, she insists that she is.

About the author

Born and raised in Edmonton Aberta, Donna Gardner has written three previous novels as the 'LateShift' Mysteries.

With a Degree in Social Work, she is a Certified Play Therapist, a consultant in Behaviour Manageement and is also a Registered Practical Nurse.

She lives in southern Ontario with her husband Paul, a German Shepherd name Sasha and Thomas the cat.

To learn more about Donna and her novels visit her website.

donnagardner.net